MICHAEL REID

VERSES OF DESIRE: ALL I EVER WANTED, NOW YOU'RE GONE

FABLED PUBLISHING

FABLED PUBLISHING

"INSPIRATIONAL NARRATIVES, PUBLISHING LEGENDS, ONE PAGE AT A TIME, CULTIVATING CREATIVITY, CRAFTING FABLED LEGENDS".

A UNIQUE INDEPENDENT PUBLISHER BASED IN THE UK WITH A GLOBAL PRESENCE. AT FABLED PUBLISHING, WE BELIEVE THAT EVERY STORY DESERVES TO BE TOLD WITH PASSION, PRECISION, AND A TOUCH OF MYSTIC MAGIC. NESTLED IN THE HEART OF THE UK, WE ARE AN ILLUMINATING BEACON FOR AUTHORS AND READERS ALIKE, DEDICATED TO BRINGING EXCEPTIONAL NARRATIVES TO LIFE TRANSFORMING AND ELEVATING MANUSCRIPTS TRANSCENDING INTO TIMELESS CLASSICS WITHSTANDING THE TEST OF TIME.

EVERY MANUSCRIPT WE TOUCH BECOMES PART OF OUR STORIED, LEGENDARY LEGACY, FORMING PART OF THE CREATIVE ARTS BECOMING FABLED WITH TIME.

OUR JOURNEY IS ONE OF CREATIVITY, INNOVATION, AND UNWAVERING COMMITMENT TO THE CREATIVE ARTS. PUBLISHING A VARIETY OF NOVELS,

SCREENPLAYS, POETRY AND VARIOUS OTHER CREATIVE PIECES FOR ASPIRATIONAL AUTHORS RIGHT ACROSS THE GLOBE. OUR APPROACH TO PUBLISHING IS UNIQUE, UTILIZING PARTNERSHIPS TO DELIVER THE BEST VALUE WITH A FOCUS ON THE AUTHOR AND THE PURPOSE OF THEIR WORK FIRST. OUR GOAL IS TO CONTINUE PUSHING BOUNDARIES, NURTURING TALENT, AND PUBLISHING STORIES THAT RESONATE WITH AUDIENCES FAR AND WIDE, FROM DEBUT NOVELISTS TO SEASONED WRITERS, WE ARE COMMITTED TO HELPING OUR AUTHORS ACHIEVE THEIR GOALS, REACHING THEIR FULL POTENTIAL.

AT FABLED PUBLISHING, OUR STEADFAST COMMITMENT TO STORYTELLING EXTENDS BEYOND TRADITIONAL FICTION AND CREATIVE WRITING. WE RECOGNIZE THE PROFOUND IMPACT OF JOURNALISM IN SHAPING PUBLIC DISCOURSE, INFORMING COMMUNITIES, AND UNCOVERING TRUTHS. THROUGH OUR DEDICATED JOURNALISM DIVISION, WE UPHOLD THE PRINCIPLES OF ACCURACY, INTEGRITY, AND ETHICAL REPORTING. HARNESSING THE POWER OF WRITTEN AND SPOKEN WORDS, WE STRIVE TO HOLD WRONGDOERS ACCOUNTABLE,

UNCOVERING TRUTHS. A QUESTIONING VOICE OFTEN INSPIRES PROFOUND THOUGHTS, SWAYING HEARTS AND MINDS, MOBILIZING PEOPLE TOWARDS ACTION, SPARKING LASTING CHANGE IN PROFOUND WAYS. EVERY SUCCESS, A TRUTHFUL TESTAMENT TO THE POWER OF A VOICE.

WE DELIVER EXCEPTIONAL, PROVOKING NARRATIVES THAT WILL WITHSTAND THE MANY TESTS OF TIME.

Contributors

We extend our heartfelt gratitude to everyone who contributed to the creation of Verses of Desire: All I Ever Wanted; Now You're Gone.

A special thank you to Lesla Traynor for designing the brilliant cover that perfectly captures the essence of our novel. We also deeply appreciate our editors for their meticulous attention to detail and the dedication they poured into shaping this story. Your efforts have made this novel an exceptional experience for our readers.

To our contributing writers, your creativity and unique voices have enriched this collection in immeasurable ways. We are grateful for your talent and commitment, which have brought this project to life with such depth and resonance.

Thank you all for being a vital part of this journey.

THE STORY

TO FULLY APPRECIATE THE ESSENCE OF THE UNIQUE GIRL WHO INSPIRED THE POEMS WITHIN THIS COLLECTION, IT IS IMPORTANT TO EXPLORE THE NARRATIVE FOUNDATIONS LAID IN MY EARLIER WORKS. "NOW YOU'RE GONE" AND "ALL I EVER WANTED" SET THE STAGE, EACH BOOK OFFERING GLIMPSES INTO HER CHARACTER AND THE WORLD SURROUNDING HER. ALTHOUGH I HAD ENVISIONED A CONCEPT OF WHO SHE WAS BEFORE COMPLETING "NOW YOU'RE GONE," IT WASN'T UNTIL AFTER THAT BOOK'S COMPLETION THAT I TRULY MET HER IN THE FLESH. ALL I EVER WANTED HITS AT HER MORE, WHILE "THE FINAL PULSE" THEN DEEPENS THE EMOTIONAL LANDSCAPE DEEPLY, SHEDDING LIGHT ON THE EXPERIENCES THAT BROUGHT HER STORY TO LIFE. ENGAGING WITH THESE PRECEDING VOLUMES WILL PROVIDE A RICHER UNDERSTANDING OF THE NUANCED INSPIRATION BEHIND THIS COLLECTION OF POEMS. TOGETHER, THEY WEAVE A HEART-FELT COMPREHENSIVE TAPESTRY OF NARRATIVE AND EMOTION, CULMINATING IN THE VERSES YOU ARE ABOUT TO DISCOVER.

COVER DESIGN
LESLA TRAYNOR

CONTRIBUTIONS FROM OTHER AUTHORS
IN COLLABORATION WITH MIKE REID.

CINDY ROSALIE – YOU NEVER KNEW
CINDY ROSALIE – ALWAYS THE SAME
SABINE TAASA – I HAD TO LET GO
MAGDALENA NASIC – BITTERSWEET MEMORIES
NATAHSA CLAIRE – HOW DID WE PART

NOVELS
MORE FROM THE AUTHOR

NOW YOU'RE GONE
ALL I EVER WANTED
CRASH AND BURN
MAKING BRITAIN GREAT AGAIN
CAREER LIFE AND PERSONAL DEVELOPMENT
CLARA ROMANOV I – TRUTH WILL UNFOLD
CLARA ROMANOV II – DECEPTION UNVEILED
CRIMELORDS - INTERVENTION

PRAISE FOR
VERSES OF DESIRE

STEPHEN MCDONALD

"A MESMERIZING COLLECTION THAT WEAVES TOGETHER PROFOUND EMOTION AND LYRICAL BEAUTY—*VERSES OF DESIRE* IS A TRUE MASTERPIECE".

LEWIS MCGREGOR

"AN EXQUISITE JOURNEY THROUGH THE LANDSCAPE OF LONGING AND LOVE; *VERSES OF DESIRE* CAPTIVATES WITH EVERY PAGE."

CLAIRE DUNCAN

"RICHLY EVOCATIVE AND BEAUTIFULLY CRAFTED, *VERSES OF DESIRE* ENCHANTS READERS WITH ITS POIGNANT STORYTELLING AND STUNNING IMAGERY."

DERVENT HART

"WITH ITS POWERFUL PROSE AND DEEP RESONANCE, *VERSES OF DESIRE* IS AN UNFORGETTABLE EXPLORATION OF THE HUMAN HEART."

LYNN KINGSTON

"A COMPELLING AND BEAUTIFULLY WRITTEN NOVEL, *VERSES OF DESIRE* CAPTURES THE ESSENCE OF DESIRE AND LOSS WITH GRACE AND INTENSITY."

Titles

I Loved And I Lost

I loved and I lost.
I fell for her once; she fell for me twice.
She was a priority, but she never felt it,
Never an option, always my choice.
I did my best, but it just wasn't enough.
She meant the world to me; I think she
knew.
I wanted more, but she could never know.
I had to let go, she had to go.

Our commitments were day and night,
She was younger, I was older.
I was cold, she was hot,
I was winter, she was summer.
I was a tundra, she a desert.
I didn't have much time, she had plenty of
time.
Our times were different, but wouldn't
always be.
Our journeys different, the destination
the same.
Change and time, one in the same.

Choices and chances, not one and the
same,

I OPENED UP, EMOTIONS FILLED THE WORDS.
I KNEW HOW I FELT, SHE DIDN'T KNOW WHAT SHE
WAS FEELING.
I KNEW IN TIME, SHE KNEW TOO.
THE THINGS WE COULD DO, THAT WE DIDN'T DO
BEFORE
TIMES HAD CHANGED, OR SO I THOUGHT.

WE FELL, BUT NOT BY CHOICE.
I PUSHED AWAY, AND I STAYED AWAY.
THE PAIN WAS TOO MUCH, I COULDN'T COPE.
I STAYED AWAY, NOT FOR ME BUT FOR HER.
I DIDN'T WANT TO, BUT I HAD TO,
LETTING HER GO, NOT FOR ME BUT FOR HER.

TWO FLAMES, ONE STILL BURNS, THE OTHER
GONE OUT.
TIME, CAN BRING THE OTHER BACK,
IN TIME, BOTH CAN BE THE SAME AGAIN.
BACK THEN I DIDN'T KNOW, BUT NOW I DO,
TIME ISN'T KIND, AS I LEARNED...

AN EMBER BURNS FOR NOW, BUT FOR HOW
LONG?
LIGHT MUST FADE TO DARK; DARKNESS CAN
BECOME LIGHT,
BUT TIME, BRINGS CHANGE.

TWO CAN BECOME ONE, IF THEY BUT MEET.
OUR LIVES COULD BOND, BECOMING ONE.
I KNEW, BUT DID SHE KNOW?

I WANTED HER, SHE WANTED ME.
SHE WAS MINE, AND I WAS HERS.
WHAT SHE WANTED, I WANTED TOO.
I WASN'T READY, BUT NOW I AM.
SHE KNEW A PART OF ME, BUT NEVER THE WHOLE.
SHE KNEW ME WHEN I WASN'T MYSELF, BUT NOW I
AM.

WHAT HAPPENED BEFORE DIDN'T HAPPEN AGAIN.
MEMORIES DANCE LIKE SHADOWS, REMINDING
ME OF WHAT WE ONCE HAD.
ECHOES OF YOUR VOICE LINGER, YET I KNOW IT
CAN'T BE.
YOUR BLOOD WILL BURN YOU; YOUR FRIENDS
WILL NOT.
IT WASN'T MY FAULT, NOR WAS IT HERS.
I DID WHAT I HAD TO DO, NOT FOR ME BUT FOR
HER....
YET IN MOMENTS OF SILENCE, I STILL WONDER,
IF SOMEONE OUR PATHS MIGHT CROSS ONCE
MORE.
AND OUR LOVE'S LOST FLAME COULD BE
RESTORED...

I Had To Let Go

Like the sun that begins its day,
While the moon but wishes to stay,
Life got in the way of you and me,
Always wishing for what could have
been.
I'd lost all hope and dreams;
The idea of us, I had to set free.

I had to let go for you to shine bright,
You're beyond my reach, but still in sight
I can't hold out; for you might not come
back to me
Your forever in my heart and mind.
Like a broken branch, not growing but
falling of a tree,
Forever wandering about what could be.
Will it truly ever end.

In my heart is where you'll always remain,
In the song of life, you're my favorite
refrain.
Even if it's the last thing I will do,
I will never stop caring for you.
For the times we shared are forever a
part of me.

YOU NEVER KNEW

MY FEELINGS STUCK TO YOU LIKE GLUE,
BUT I DON'T THINK YOU EVER KNEW.
WHETHER I LOVED YOU OR NOT, TO YOU IT WAS
ALWAYS A MYSTERY-
THAT'S WHY THERE'S NO "FOREVER", THERE'S
ONLY A FADING HISTORY.
IN YOUR EYES, I SOUGHT A REFLECTION OF MY
TRUTH, YET FOUND ONLY UNCERTAINTY.

LOVE CAN BE SIMPLE, LIKE ONE, TWO, THREE,
BUT IF IT'S NOT, YOU SET THE OTHER FREE.
YOU REALLY TRUSTED IN OUR KIND OF
ROMANCE.
AND GAVE ME A SECOND CHANCE.
BUT THINGS CHANGED, BUT NOT FOR ME-
THINGS WEREN'T RIGHT, THEY WEREN'T WHAT I
WANTED.
I DID MY BEST, BUT IT JUST WASN'T ENOUGH.
YOU HAD TO FLY, WHILE I STAYED PUT.
I WAS LEFT TO NAVIGATE THE TURBULENT SEA,
YOU LEFT.
YET NOW IT CRASHES UPON THE SHORES OF
WHAT COULD HAVE BEEN.
I AM WAITING ON MY THREE, BUT HOW WILL I
KNOW?

You deserve more than you could ever imagine,
Not being able to love you now feels like a sin.
You meant the world to me, but now you're just a dream.
Some people look for the drama,
But love's end sometimes feels like karma.

Right now, I feel like I'll regret this for the rest of my life-
I was your first boyfriend, but you'll be another man's wife.
Love's not supposed to show us what we want, but what we need.
You said all you needed was me, and I you.
But next to you, there's a "reserved" note on the seat.
We wanted each other, but needed something else.
And that's the kind of story fate tells.
A different path fate wrote for us to meet.
Lost in the pages of time, yet we may one day again meet.

You were all I ever wanted, and now you're gone.

ANOTHER NOT TO BE

I FOUND ANOTHER, OR SO I THOUGHT.
WE SHARED A SHOWER, BUT SOMETHING JUST
DIDN'T FEEL RIGHT.
IT WASN'T WARM, IT WAS COLD.
IT WASN'T RIGHT, IT WAS WRONG.
SOMETHING JUST WASN'T THEIR
I WAS THEIR BUT MY MIND ELSEWHERE.
WHAT I FELT BEFORE, JUST WASN'T THEIR
NOT WITH HER, BUT WITH ANOTHER
THAT WAS THEN, THIS IS NOW.
I CALLED IT OFF, IT COULDN'T GO ON.
IT COULD HAVE GONE ON, BUT I HAD TO SAY
NO.
IF IT'S NOT THERE, YOU MOVE ON
A CONNECTION'S BOTH WAYS, NOT JUST ONE...
LOVE WASN'T THERE, IT WAS ELSEWHERE.
WHAT WAS THIS, WAS I LOVING ANOTHER?

I SHOULDN'T CARE, BUT I STILL DO.
I SHOULDN'T CARE, YET I STILL CARE.
TWO YEARS HAVE PASSED, TIMES MOVED ON,
HOW CAN I NOT HAVE MOVED ON?
I THOUGHT I HAD, YET SHE'S DAWNED UPON ME
AGAIN,

Suddenly, without warning, its happened again,
This is the second time without warning,
she's resonated once more.
This is the second time.
Why is she back? It doesn't make sense.
Will she forever be, in my heart and mind?
Haunted by memories I thought I left
behind.
She lingers still, her resonance echoing
down the corridors of time.
Can I ever truly let go? I am not in
control.
Can I ever break free from this pain?
Can I be set free to love again.

It was over long ago, but I hadn't yet let
go.
She was gone long ago, I never let go.
In the mirror I see only me, not the way I
wanted things to be.
Time had passed by, but not for me.
What I felt, I will never feel again for
What is rare, is not easily found
I will keep searching, but I may never find.
For time wasn't my friend, it hadn't been
for a long time.

THE DAYS TURNED TO YEARS, YET THE ACHE REMAINS THE SAME.

I WAS DRAWN BACK, BUT FOR WHY I COULDN'T UNDERSTAND.

I HAVE QUESTIONS, THINGS I NEED TO KNOW—SHE HOLDS THE ANSWERS.

SHE FELL FOR ME TWICE, BUT I ONLY FELL FOR HER ONCE.

SHE WAS ALL I EVER WANTED, BUT WAS I HERS?

SHE SAID IT HERSELF, ALL SHE EVER WANTED WAS JUST ME, ALL WE COULD HAVE DONE THAT SHALL NEVER BE.

I THOUGHT A DOOR WAS OPEN, HOWEVER, IT WAS THEN CLOSED.

MAYBE IT REALLY WAS JUST NOW ONLY ME.

WHAT I WANTED, WASN'T TO BE

IN THE ABSENCE OF LIGHT IN THE DARK OF NIGHT, YOUR ABSENCE WHISPERS LOUDLY.

I HAVE TO LET GO; I HAVE TO MOVE ON

THE SUDDEN RISE OF FEELINGS AGAIN FOR HER, CANNOT BE EXPLAINED.

FOR THIS IS SECOND TIME, THIS HAS HAPPENED TO ME.

WAS IT UNFINISHED BUSINESS, A CHANCE I WOULD NOW NEVER GET?

TIMES HAVE TRULY CHANGED NOT FOR ME, YET NOW WE'LL NEVER KNOW. SHE WAS ALL I EVER WANTED, NOW YOU'RE GONE...

TIME

I SHOULDN'T CARE, YET I STILL DO.
TWO YEARS HAVE PASSED, TIME HAS MOVED ON,
I HAVE TO LET GO; I HAVE TO MOVE ON, YET.
"SHE HAS DARTED BACK INTO MY HEART."
BUT MAYBE SHE NEVER REALLY LEFT.
A VOID RESIDES WITHIN ME.
I NEVER LET GO, FOR WHAT I DESIRED FOR US,
WE NEVER HAD THE CHANCE.
UNFINISHED BUSINESS REMAINS.
IN THE SILENCE, HER ABSENCE ECHOES.
I'M LEFT GRAPPLING WITH MEMORIES THAT
REFUSE TO FADE.

MY MIND IS CLOUDED, SHE IS THEIR TOO.
WHY IS SHE BACK? IT MAKES NO SENSE.
MEMORIES HAUNT LIKE RELENTLESS SHADOWS,
REFUSING TO FADE.
I CANNOT GO ON; THE PAIN IS SO MUCH.
HOW CAN I MOVE FORWARD, WHILE BURDENED
BY THE PAST?
I COULD FIGHT, BUT WHAT WOULD BE THE
POINT? TOO MUCH TIME HAS GONE, IT WILL
NEVER BE THE SAME.
WILL SHE EVER FEEL THE SAME?

HER DISTANT PRESENCE REMAINS, A WHISPER IN THE WINDS CARRIED BY TIME,
UNANSWERED QUESTIONS REMAIN, LINGERING IN THE SHADOWS OF MY HEART AND MIND.
I CAN'T GET HER OUT THE MAZE OF MY MIND.
SHE'S A PUZZLE OCCUPYING THE CHAMBERS OF MY MIND, YET TO BE SOLVED.
HER PRESENCE REMAINS A MYSTERY I CANNOT DECIPHER, SOME ANSWERS ARE LOST TO THE BOOKS OF TIME.

WHAT CAN A SIMPLE GUY DO?
I MUST CARRY THESE MEMORIES WITH A HEAVY HEART, FOR THEIR SACRED MORE SO THAN PRECIOUS GOLD. THESE WILL NEVER FADE AWAY ONLY ON MY LAST DAY, WILL THEY FADE WITH ME.
WHY NOW AND WHY ME? TIME ISN'T MERCIFUL.
I CANNOT REACH OUT, AS TIME HAS MOVED ON.
SHE HAS MOVED ON, YET I HAVE NOT.
I'M UNABLE TO GIVE UP, YET I CANNOT FIGHT.
SHE WAS ALL I EVER WANTED, AND NOW SHE'S GONE.
I WILL KEEP ON FIGHTING UNTIL I DIE, FOR SHE SHALL FOREVER BE A PART OF ME, YET.
I FEEL SHE SHALL NEVER KNOW, HOW MUCH SHE MEANT TO ME...

Part Of Me

She knew me when I wasn't myself.
She knew me when I was low and down.
She knew me when life was difficult.
She knew me but not fully nor truly.
Yet she loved me still...
When I pulled away, she pulled me back.
I wanted so much, but she could never know.
I had to let go, not for my sake but for her.
It was a mortal wound, for it would never to heal, even with time.

In time, I reached out again when days were brighter.
I told her how I felt, she didn't know what she was feeling.
Eventually, we both felt the same.
I feel for her once, she fell for me twice.
She knew I cared for her deeply, but did she truly see it?
Actions speak more than words, however sometimes they fall short.
I gave it my all, but it just wasn't enough.

FOR CIRCUMSTANCES CHANGED AGAIN, I DID
ALL I COULD...
SHE DIDN'T ASK FOR MUCH, ALL SHE EVER
WANTED WAS JUST MY TIME, FOR WHICH I
COULDN'T GIVE.
WE TRIED HOWEVER,
SHE COULDN'T COPE, IN TIME SHE LET ME GO.
IT'S A WRONG, I'LL NEVER MAKE RIGHT.

A DOOR REMAINED OPEN, OR SO I BELIEVED.
I WANTED TO BE KIND AND STAY AWAY.
I DIDN'T WANT TO REACH BACK OUT AGAIN.
FOR I DO NOT HAVE THE HEART, SHE
SHOULDN'T FEEL THAT WAY AGAIN.
WOULD SHE EVER FEEL THE SAME WAY I FELT
ABOUT HER, WOULD SHE EVER REACH OUT TO
ME?
COULD WE RECLAIM, WHAT WE ONCE SHARED?
WOULD SHE FEEL THE WAY I FELT FOR HER
AGAIN, I DON'T KNOW?
I REACHED OUT AGAIN, ONLY FOR A COLD
EMBRACE.
IT'S BEEN TOO LONG I CANNOT FIGHT; TIME HAS
MOVED ON SHE WILL HAVE MOVED ON.
WHAT WAS THERE IS NOW NO LONGER THEIR

She never knew the full me, she only knew a part of me.
Part of me refrained for I could see what she truly needs.
So much remained unsaid,
A fragile balance exerted, and overtime fell to dust.
We were one in wants and desires, yet we now stumbled and faltered.
Dreams turned to shadows; the light fell to dark.
I felt our flame would burn again, lighting the way.
For us to meet in the maze of life.
Shadows would be cast aside when our time comes, to meet again.
Convergence is destined to dawn again.
A flame will burn again, showing us the way through the maze of life, like the guiding of a compass or mapping of stars.

I feel she is now gone; she was all I ever wanted.
I long for one last chance, to know if we could be.
I will keep on fighting until I die, for she shall forever be a part of me...

Commitment

I made an effort; it was the best I could give.
She wanted more; but I was unable to give.
She was longing for more, I wanted more,
But I couldn't change the tides, I committed,
Knowing the tides can change.
I just needed to buy some time, as time brings
change.
Like an anchor, steadying us through life's
unpredictable tides.
I never lost hope, for the way we connected
defies the very laws of time.

I travelled across the country to see her,
after gruelling twelve-hour days.
Enduring over three hours of travel, just to
be near her.
A journey to my hearts solace.
I stayed over, yet when I wanted to go, she
didn't want me to leave.
But I had departed, for reasons beyond my
control.
I was her first boyfriend, she's the first women
I really fell for.
I wanted so much, yet I couldn't ever show it.
Our time together, felt like stolen moments.
A hidden haven, where time itself paused for
only us.
Nature itself bowed to our love.

WE WERE SAFE YET, BUT WE EMBRACED IT RISKY.
I FELT SO STRONGLY FOR HER DEEPLY, DRIVEN BY AN INTENSE PASSION,
THAT IF SOMETHING AROSE FROM IT, I WOULD DO WHATEVER I HAD TO DO FOR HER,
I COULD WALK ON WATER OR MOVE MOUNTAINS,
EVEN THE GODS WOULD HEAR MY CRY,
NO ASK WOULD BE DENIED.
I PROMISED MYSELF I WOULD ALWAYS BE HERS, NO MATTER WHAT.
NO FORCE OF NATURE COULD TEAR US APART.

AFTERWARDS, WE SHARED A SHOWER, IT WAS PURE BLISS.
I CUDDLED HER, HELD HER CLOSE, MY ARMS WERE AROUND HER- IT WAS BREATHTAKING.
SHE EMBRACED ME AS I EMBRACED HER,
IN THOSE TENDER MOMENTS, WE WERE THE OTHERS WORLD.
THE WARMTH WE FELT WAS UNLIKE ANY OTHER,
THAT MOMENT WE DIDN'T WANT TO END, SHE FELT IT AS DID I.
I WAS HERS AND SHE WAS MINE.
SHE WAS ALL I EVER WANTED, WHILE I WAS ALL SHE EVER WANTED.
IN THAT MOMENT, WE KNEW WE WERE MEANT TO BE, OUR DESTINIES INTERTWINED,
NOT AN ACT OF GOD, BUT BY EXISTENCES GRAND DESIGN.
OUR HEARTS AND MINDS ALIGNED.

BLOOD WILL BURN

I WAS SCALDED, I WAS BURNT.
THEY'LL TAKE IT ALL, WITHOUT REGARD.
THEY'LL EXPECT MORE FROM YOU THAN THEY'D
ASK OF ANOTHER.
I DID MORE TO THAN THEY DID, YET THEY'D ASK
FOR MORE.
THEY WILL TAKE AND NOT RECIPROCATE,
ASSUME RATHER THAN KNOW.
IS IT AN EXPECTATION, OR SIMPLY WHAT YOU
ENDURE?
BLOOD LOSS TAKES A HEAVY TOLL, ON US ALL.
FOR YOUR BLOOD IS A PART OF YOU.

I WORKED HARDER, I DID MORE FOR MY
SHOULDERS WERE BURDENED.
WITH RESPONSIBILITIES THAT WERE NOT MINE.
I PUSHED AND CARRIED ON, DOING WHAT I
MUST DO FOR MYSELF.
I BATTLED AND SOLDIERED ON, WOULDN'T LOSE,
I CARRIED ON.
IT TOOK ITS TOLL, BUT NOT ON ME, BUT ON
ANOTHER.
IT WASN'T FAIR, I DID THE BEST THAT I COULD,
BUT IT JUST WASN'T ENOUGH.

ONCE THIS SIGNIFICANT OTHER WAS HURTING,
IT CHANGED ME.
I HAD TO SAY NO, THIS COULDN'T GO ON.

IT WASN'T OUR FIRST TIME; IT WAS OUR SECOND
TIME.
A SECOND CHANCE TO DO, WHAT I ALWAYS
WANTED US TO BE.
AN OPPORTUNITY FOR WHAT WE DREAMED,
UNFORTUNATELY, THAT WAS NOT TO BE, FOR I
WAS UNABLE TO DO ALL I WANTED US TO BE.
SHE NEEDED MORE, THAN I COULD GIVE; IT WAS
TEARING US APART.
EVENTUALLY THE STRAIN BECAUSE TOO MUCH,
OUR DREAMS TURNED TO DUST.
IT WAS A STEP BACK, INTO THE PAST,
SOMEWHERE I DIDN'T WANT US TO BE.
FOR IT WASN'T OUR BEST TIME, BAD THOUGHTS
AND EXPERIENCES LINGERED.

SHE FELT AN INCONVENIENCE, THIS WAS NEVER
THE CASE.
FOR I HAD REACHED OUT TO HER, FOR I CARED
DEEPLY.
PART OF ME WAS VOID, WITHOUT HER GUIDING
LIGHT, I WOULD BE IN DARKNESS.

There was nothing more I could do; it just wasn't fair.

Would I get a third chance? I don't think there will be, was the response.

Yet I held out hope, hoping for what happened before, it was not to be.

Our past had burned what we could have been.

Your blood will burn you, your friends shall not.

I learned I had loved, and I had truly lost in time.

It wasn't my fault, nor was it hers for wanting me, the way I wanted her.

I feel as though she never knew how much she meant to me.

Echoes of our past our dreams still linger, emerging from shadows without steps of announcement.

Taunting me always, for they never truly fade... a constant reminder that,

I will keep on fighting until I die, for she was a part of me, and I her.

I will try again for times have truly changed, if she but picks up the phone again...

Lost Opportunities

That fateful day, long ago,
When she tried to get me to stay,
The way she did it, changed it all.
The puppy dog eyes staring through me-
I was unsure what to do.
If I went, she'd be hurt.
If I stayed, she'd be hurt too,
What's a guy supposed to do?
It made me think this isn't right,
I needed time.
This step back changed it all.

I did my best to see her, but it was never enough.
You can't complain for ones commitment to you.
The dreams I wanted for us remained unachievable.
Almost within reach, forever slipping away.
I could almost reach out and grab them, yet they'd move further away.
She relived the past.
I just needed more time.
She was already struggling.

I WANTED SO MUCH, YET SHE COULD NEVER
KNOW.
I COULD SEE WHAT I WANTED, REMAINING JUST
OUT OF REACH.
I WANTED FAMILY, I WANTED KIDS, BUT I JUST
WASN'T AT THE RIGHT PLACE IN TIME.
I COULDN'T LOSE HER,
IF I DID, THERE'D BE NO THIRD CHANCE.

THAT STEP BACK, CHANGED IT ALL.
IT HURT HER DEEPLY, DESPITE MY
REASSURANCES.
BY THE TIME WE TALKED, SHE WAS ALREADY
GONE.
IN TIME, IT WILL ALL PASS, BUT HOW LONG MUST
I WAIT?
I'M LETTING GO OF HOPE,
YET I DON'T WANT IT TO END THIS WAY.

IS THIS THE WAY IT'S MEANT TO BE?
I PROMISED MYSELF, YOU PROMISED ME.
WE SAID IT OURSELVES; WE WERE MEANT TO BE.
THIS JUST DOESN'T FEEL RIGHT.
YOU AND I NOW PARTING WAYS.
GOING OUR SEPARATE WAYS
WERE WE MEANT TO BE?
IS THERE TRULY NO OTHER WAY?

We were like stars in the sky, always there for the other.
Our bond shimmered like the northern lights, ethereal and timeless.
We needed no compass to find the other.
The stars shined brightly on you; I always knew the path to you.
I thought we would never crash and burn.
However, all good things must come to an end.
For even stars fade and fall, their light turning to dark.
But a distant glow in the night sky,
A reminder of what once was.
But could never be again.
Yet our memories withstand the tests of time,
The universe is infinite, just like where you and I could have gone.
A voice still echoes long after the big bang's birth,
Stars show us the path we could not yet follow,
Maybe in time, what was, could be again...
A new dawn may show the path for our hearts to once more align.

Wants And Life

I loved her so much, I had to let her go,
Not for me, but for her- she could never
know.
I got a hard fought second chance.
It was an unpredictable advance.
She was never an option; she was the only
chance.
Life changed again; we parted ways.
Circumstances of the day dictated our
separate days.
We had to part ways, though it was never
by choice.

She fell for me twice, I fell only once,
The moment I saw you, I feel into a trance.
Each time, our hearts intertwined.
Time had passed, feelings remained strong
and intense.
Would I get a third chance, I wondered.
We shared something, not but once but
twice.
We had something not but once but
twice.
Fate intervened, our paths misaligned,

It simply wasn't to be, I reached out, only to be shot back down.
Hope was turned upside down.

I wanted you more than you could ever know.
Maybe I should have told you everything from the moment we met, but I could not.
From the moment we met, to the moment you left,
It was a departing blow.
A part of me walked away from me that day.
You meant everything to me.
All I ever wanted was for us to be.
In my heart and mind, you remain within reach.

Yet our differences kept us apart.
For you were younger, I was older.
Our times different.
My past kept me unable to fully commit to you.
If given the time, this would change.
For we could rearrange, bridging the gap to another.

I WANTED YOU AND ME LIVE TOGETHER,
TO RAISE KIDS TOGETHER, JUST AS YOU WISHED
ON THAT FATEFUL DAY.
I ENVISIONED US GROWING OLD TOGETHER.
IN A COSY PLACE THAT WE CALL OUR OWN.
TO WAKE UP TOGETHER, JUST LIKE WE USED TO.
TO HAVE A DOG AND A HORSE, OUR DREAMS
TIED TOGETHER.
WHERE MY FRIENDS ARE YOURS, AND YOURS
ARE MINE.
I WANTED TO STAND BY THE ALTER, WAITING
FOR YOU TO COME TO ME,
FOR OUR FAMILIES TO UNITE AND INTERTWINE,
OUR LIVES FOREVER ENTWINED.

IN EVERY PART OF LIFE, I SAW US SIDE BY SIDE.
FOREVER BUILDING A LIFE TOGETHER, FOREVER
ALIGNED.

YOU SHALL FOREVER BE IN MY HEART AND
MIND,
THE TIMES WE SHARED MEANT SOMETHING TO
US BOTH.
I WILL KEEP ON FIGHTING UNTIL I DIE,
WE WILL NEVER CRASH AND BURN,
WAITING FOR A DREAM TO COME TO LIFE,
I FOREVER WILL HOLD A DOOR OPEN FOR YOU...

Not Once But Thrice

I feel for her once, she fell for me twice.
We went separate ways, because we had
too.
I stayed away until brighter days arose.
I never wanted to lose her, the first time
yet I had too.
Not for me but for her, I cared too much
to stay.

One fateful night, a friend described the
loss of a significant other.
What he described resonated with me
igniting a fire again,
His love for another ignited a love in me,
One I'd locked away.

Feelings rose like a phoenix from the
ashes,
Swiftly quickly, like a wildfire spreading
across forests,
Burning bright an intensity nothing
could match,
The barriers around my heart, consumed
away,
Stars erupting like fireworks on new
year's eve,

Each spark a reminder of our wants and dreams.
Constellations of hope replaced the void.
You were my light in the dark.
It was like she was never gone; it was my first experience of this.
They were locked away, the key thrown away, into an unknown abyss.
I couldn't bear the weight of caring,
Knowing I could not hold you close,
Sharing in your dreams.
That fateful night changed the way things were to be.

She fell for me once more, yet it was not meant to be,
Life got in the way of you and me.
We parted ways again for, I couldn't yet commit to you the way you wanted.
Again, I stayed away, for I'd hurt you not once but twice,
It was never my intent, for I cared about you.
It wasn't me, but someone led us to a dark place and locked you away.
Again, feelings returned to the ashes.

Your flame went out again, did you
really lose your guiding light.
Or did a part of me never really let go of
the idea of you and me.

Yet time passed, undisturbed by external
voices, you rose again from the ashes.
Suddenly, without warning your guiding
light returned; what did I see.
I was barely breathing, my starlight
returned.
You were found again, I cannot explain,
for what is rare is not easily found.
I followed your guiding light, straight
to you.
I was turned away; we were out of time.
Angels weren't listening tonight, my
wishes gone unanswered.
Too much time had gone by, you were
truly gone.
In the past you were truly gone, I had not
yet realized.
Your light would not rise again.
The stars no longer aligned for us, but
time would bring change yet again...

Born To A Different Life

If I were born into wealth, what could be different?
I wouldn't need to work, nor study for a better life, an expansive canvas without limits imposed.
We could follow the sun, taking flight.

Unchained by need, I'd strive for more, reaching for the stars.
Burdens of life lifted; I could truly live.
Spending time with her, day into night, with her always by my side,
Never running away at the sun's invite,
Morning's arrival, not an awaited departure.
No worries in life, I could simply live.
Time would be my friend, not my enemy.

I could follow my dreams, instead of just dreaming.
I'd follow if I could, yet I could not.
She wouldn't have walked into darkness, out of sight and mind, she could dawn again.
Priorities shifted, like a pendulum shift.

MONEY AND TIME, NOT MY CONCERNS.
I WOULDN'T HAVE PULLED, NOR SHE PUSHED
AWAY.
WE'D HAVE ADVENTURES NOT JUST THE OTHERS
LITTLE TIME.
WE'D KNOW IF I WERE RIGHT FOR HER AND ME
HER.
UNKNOWN QUESTIONS WOULD BE ANSWERED.
SHADOWS FADE AND TRUTHS UNFOLD.
THE LIGHT BRINGING CLARITY TO ONCE
OBSCURED PATHS, WE BUT WALKED.
OUR QUESTIONS WOULD BE ANSWERED.

IN THE REALM OF AFFLUENCE, OUR
ADVENTURES ARE EXPANSIVE, LIKE EXISTENCE
ITSELF.
OUR BOND WOULD NEVER FADE, OUR
CONNECTION ETERNAL, YET A DIFFERENT LIFE
HAS BEEN LIVED.
I LEFT PONDERING OVER WHAT COULD HAVE
BEEN.
I WILL KEEP FIGHTING UNTIL I DIE, FOREVER
FORGING THE LIFE I WANTED TO LIVE.
I'LL RUN UP THE COLOSSEUM STAIRS, AND I'LL
SHAPE MY DESTINY.
CREATING THE OUTCOME I DESIRE, FOR I ALL
ALWAYS CARE ABOUT YOU.

Life's Unfairness

I wasn't bad, I wasn't good, I did the best
that a guy could.
I couldn't see her often, even when I
could,
Rare were the times I saw her face,
I couldn't do much, can you blame her?

I just wasn't enough, at that point in time.
Time couldn't fly quickly enough to save
us. I just couldn't buy enough time...

She got made one night, the way I looked
at her enraged her,
She didn't see I was hurting inside.
I saw how happy she was, yet I knew she
needed more.

Yet I knew, she needed more than what I
could provide.
Her smile was a beacon, to a place I could
not follow, my compass lost...
I pulled away, she pushed away,
A ship of time carried her away.
When time was my friend.
I would follow in time...

POWERS OF ALTERATION

IF I WERE A SUPERHERO, I WOULD TURN DAY BACK
INTO NIGHT,
I WOULD TURN BACK TIME, CHANGING THE TIDES
OF TIME.
BOOKS OF HISTORY WOULD ALTER THEIR WORDS.
THE GODS WOULD HEED MY DEMANDS,
FOR EVEN THEY SHALL DARE NOT STAND
BETWEEN US.
THEY SHALL BOW BEFORE OUR ENDURING LOVE,
THEIR DIVINE POWERS NO MATCH FOR OUR
BOND,

NATURE WOULD OBEY OUR EVERY WHIM.
THE STORM OF LIFE AND TIMES THAT CONSUMED
US, WOULD NO LONGER SINK US,
POSEIDON WOULD SHOULDER US, CARRYING US
ABOVE THE TEMPEST.
OUR LIVES PROPELLED BY NEW WINDS.
GUIDED BY OUR HEARTS COMPASS, WE WOULD
REACH NEW HEIGHTS.
ALTERING OUR FATE.
WE'D SCULPT OUR OWN FUTURE, THE SHADOWS
OF TIME NO LONGER CONSUMING US.
WE MAKE OUR OWN DESTINIES, UNCHAINED
FROM THE BURDENS OF OUR PASTS.

Unable To Write

I write, yet the plot I desire eludes me,
always escaping.
She hides at the back of mind somewhere
to be heard but never seen nor caught.
A whisper in the void of shadows,
taunting me always...

I rearrange the plot, like a great game of
chess,
Every move calculated, yet the outcome
stays the same,
No matter what I do the outcome remains
unchanged,
No path leads there, every move destined
to fail.
Sacrificing the queen, still dooms me to
failure.
I cannot bring you and I together.
Like the crossing of no man's land, it
seems and feels just not possible,
Yet I do not protest, and I continue.
For in time eventually I shall cross,
securing the outcome I seek.
I said I would always care, yet I continue
a helpless hopeless pursuit...

A Battle Lost

That day I lost you, I lost a part of me,
A part of me ran, never to be seen again.
Part of my heart and soul, carried away,
I retreated into a trench so deep, the skies
turned to darkness.
A ladder to the bottom of a well just
wouldn't reach,
I never really climbed back out.
A part of me stayed there for many years.

I was shell-shocked and lost,
A part of me stayed in the shadows, afraid
of day lights light.
For seeing it all again, would send me
back in retreat,
To the abyss in which I now sit,
Where memories never fade to shadows, a
constant of echo of what resides above.

The call to arms would be ignored,
For I was broken, I was a broken man.
A crater, a void that cannot be filled,
exists,
The dawn a reminder of what is gone, I am
consumed by the darkness.

RESIDING IN SHADOWS, I NEVER LET GO OF OUR MOMENTS, A PART OF ME GUARDS THEM.
IN SLUMBER I WRITE, TO REMIND AND REFLECT.
VALUING THE LITTLE TIME WE HAD, THEY WERE FEW BUT STRONG, STRONGER THAN DAMASCUS STEEL.
NOTHING WOULD FADE THOSE MOMENTS.
IN DARKNESS YOU ARE MY CANDLELIGHT.
PROVIDING LIGHT AND WARMTH.

I WAS DRIVEN MAD BY YOUR LOSS, THOUGH YOU WERE NEVER LOST.
I KNEW WHERE YOU WERE, I COULDN'T MESSAGE BY CARRIER PIGEON NOR A SIMPLE TEXT,
FOR MY TIMES REMAINED UNCHANGED.
THE EGO, INNER SELF MY SUBCONSCIOUS MIND PROTECTED ME, CARRYING ME AWAY ON A GREAT STRETCHER WHERE I WAS,
SURROUNDED BY VARIOUS CONSTRUCTS, OF THE INNER MINDS CREATIVE UNKNOWN.
YOU WERE LOCKED AWAY WITH ME,
FOR I COULDN'T COPE, WITHOUT YOU BY MY SIDE.
BESTOWED WITH GRIEF WORSE THAN BEING HIT BY STRAY BULLETS,
FOR I MUST LIVE WITH THIS PAIN, THE CAUSE OF WHICH STILL ELUDES ME...

TIMES HAVE TRULY CHANGED; I DON'T CARRY
THE WOUNDS OF MY PAST.
CONCERNS OF THOSE DAYS, NO LONGER
CONCERNS OF TODAY.
MY SHOULDERS UNBURDENED, A GREAT RELIEF,
THE GATES OF ESCAPE FINALLY OPENED.
I DASH OUT, KNOWING WHERE I'M HEADING.
A PART OF ME HAS REJOINED ITSELF.
NOW TIMES HAVE CHANGED, I REACHED BACK
OUT WITH SIGNALLING INTENT.

I RADIOED AHEAD; THE MESSAGE GOT
THROUGH, ONLY TO GO UNANSWERED,
TWENTY-FOUR HOURS LATER, THE RECEIVER
WENT SILENT. HER PHOTO ONCE VIBRANT, NOW
FADED TO GREY.
I WAITED HALFWAY, FOR DAYS ON THE PLAINS
BEFORE CONTINUING ON,
I CALLED INSTEAD, ONLY TO BE MET WITH COLD
INDIFFERENCE.
A FLAME THAT ONCE STALKED ME IN THE
SHADOWS THAT NEVER WENT OUT, STILL BURNS
BUT IT'S CLEAR THE OTHER HAS LONG GONE
OUT.

IT SEEMS THE PAGES WRITTEN, AN ALTERNATE
HISTORY, FOR YOU ARE TRULY LOST...

Personal Change

I focused on myself, building my wealth.
Freeing myself from the restraints of
time.
Bound no more by lack of time.
I've shed old weights, becoming stronger
and fitter once more.
I improved, both for myself and the
future
I changed; I became more resilient.
Before I but walked and cycled, now I've
shifted to driving.
Charting our own way through open
skies.
Nothing would bring our journey to an
end.
Nature herself couldn't stop us flying.

Opportunities unfold before me,
Profoundly clear on the horizon,
Our wants and dreams realised.
We can chart beyond the horizon,
Going wherever our hearts may dream.
Our journey is limitless, waiting to be
mapped out.
Infinite possibilities lie before us,

ALL THE CHANGES OF TODAY-
SHE WOULDN'T FEEL AN INCONVENIENCE.
I FEEL, SHE KNEW ME WELL.
YET SHE KNEW ME, WHEN TIME AND MONEY
WERE SCARCE.
WHEN TIME AND MONEY WERE TIGHT, THEY
KEPT US APART.
PREVENTED US FROM OUR TIME...
I COULDN'T INTERVENE, IT HAD TO UNFOLD.
NOW IS OUR TIME, TO SHINE-
CHANGE IS MOMENTOUS, NOW AN ALLY.

WHEN I REACHED OUT ONCE MORE, SHE DIDN'T
SEE THE CHANGE.
SHE DIDN'T GIVE OUR LOVE A SECOND
THOUGHT.
A VACUUM OF DESPAIR DRAINED ME TO THE
CORE.
WORDS FELL SILENT BETWEEN US, UNSPOKEN
AND FORGOTTEN.

IT SEEMS TIME HAS CHANGED HER TOO.
I NEED TO KNOW, YET I CAN NEVER KNOW.
TIME HAS PASSED, AS IT INEVITABLY DOES.
WE GREW, DIVERGING WITH PASSAGE OF TIME.
I FOREVER LIVE IN REGRET, FOR WHAT MIGHT
HAVE BEEN...

DECEPTION

YOU CHEAT YOU STEAL YOU FEEL ENTITLED TO
THAT WHICH ISN'T YOURS.
YOU BORROW AND TAKE WITHOUT REGARD,
YOU LOOK UPON ME AS A BANK, TURNING MY
POCKETS INSIDE OUT.
YOU PUSH ONE INTO THE RED, A PLACE I
SHOULDN'T BE.
YOU LEFT ME HOLDING ONTO THE EDGE,
YOUR PROMISES NOW DELUSIONS .
RESPECT IS EARNED, NOT GIVEN FREELY.
WHAT YOU TOOK FROM ME CAN NEVER BE
REGAINED-
FOR WHAT IS RARE IS NOT EASILY FOUND.
I LOST SOME DEAR BECAUSE OF YOU.

I HAD A GOOD JOB, IT WASN'T ENOUGH.
I COULDN'T EARN ENOUGH, NO MATTER WHAT.
WHAT WAS TAKEN WASN'T RETURNED IN TIME.
I COULDN'T DO MORE, IT WAS HER TIME.
I LOVED AND I THEN LOST,
HAD DECEPTION AND DECEIT NOT BEEN USED,
WE MIGHT STILL BE ALRIGHT.
I CAN'T TURN BACK TIME.
I FEEL OUR TIME WAS TRULY BURNED,
HAD I NOT TRUSTED IN ONE.

WAS I WRONG

WAS IT RIGHT OR WAS IT WRONG?
SHE SHUT ME OUT, A SUDDEN SURPRISE.
FOR DOUBTS OR FEARS, I'D NEVER KNOW,
SHE DID WHAT I NEVER THOUGHT SHE'D DO.
SHE BLOCKED ME OUT OF HER LIFE.

AM I THE BETTER ONE, IN THE LIGHT?
FOR I'D NEVER DO, DO WHAT SHE HAS JUST
DONE.
I'VE MAINTAINED MY IMAGE, JUST AND BRIGHT,
WHILE HERS HAS COME UNDONE.

SHE'S LOST HER STANDING IN MY EYES,
FOR TREATING PEOPLE RIGHT ISN'T HARD,
TALKING ISN'T THAT HARD.
BEING FAIR AND KIND ISN'T THAT HARD.

IF OUR POSITIONS WERE REVERSED,
AT LEAST I'D BE FAIR AND SIMPLY TALK.
NO HARM COMES FROM A TALK,
SOMETIMES ONE SIMPLY NEEDS TO KNOW!
I'D MANAGE HER WISHES, BEST I COULD.
I WOULDN'T LEAVE HER NOT KNOWING.
NOR IN PAIN,
LIKE SHE HAS DONE TO ME

STANDING IN HER SHOES,
I SEE WHAT SHE HAS SEEN.
I WOULD FIGHT NIGHT AND DAY FOR HER.
WOULD SHE DO THE SAME FOR ME?
WOULD SHE FEEL THE WAY I FELT?
AND FINALLY UNDERSTAND THE HORROR
OF WHAT SHE HAS DONE?

AM I THE MORE CARING ONE?
IN TIME, WOULD I STILL FIGHT?
WITH THE PASSING OF TIME PEOPLE CHANGE.
WOULD I RECONCILE, OR TURN AWAY?
I SIMPLY DON'T KNOW...

CAN I FORGIVE?
I SIMPLY DON'T KNOW.
SHE IS TEARING ME APART.
HOW CAN I SEE HER AGAIN?
WOULD I INVITE HER BACK INTO MY LIFE WITH
OPEN ARMS, OR TURN HER AWAY?
WOULD I FORGIVE AND FORGET,
OR HOLD HER IN CONTEMPT?
FOR I'D NEVER DO WHAT SHE DID TO ME.
I CARED TOO MUCH, TO DO SUCH A THING.
AT ONE POINT, SHE DID TOO.
THE FUTURE HOLDS THE ANSWERS TO SPOKEN
QUESTIONS.

A Rare Gem

She was cute, untouched perfection.
She shone bright like a diamond.
Rare, genuine, and pure
Her desires glistened blissful intensions.
Her heart was pure as were her intensions.
I saw my reflection glistening in her eyes.
The way we she smiled at me; I knew she was happy with me.
Her touch soft and gentle, showing her care.
Together we embraced a love that felt like a rare gem, hidden and hard to find.
Moments with her were timeless treasures.
Moments together were sheer perfection.
A treasure I carry to this day,
The way we connected, was pure and true.
I felt it as did she.
I had no hidden intent, my love was clear.
I was her first boyfriend; she was the first woman I every truly fell for
But it just wasn't the right time,
I had to push away, she deserved better.
The best I could do, just wouldn't be enough.

I HAD TO WALK AWAY, SURRENDERING HOPES
AND DREAMS.
A PART OF ME BECAME BURIED AND LOST THAT
VERY DAY.
DARKNESS CLOUDED THAT WHICH WAS LEFT
BEHIND.
SOMETHING BURNED IN THE SHADOWS,
YET I DID NOT KNOW IT.
DIVINE INTERVENTION STRIPPED THE SHADOWS
AWAY.
WHAT POWER INTERVENED I DO NOT KNOW;
THEY DIDN'T HELP ME?
HAD I ANGERED THE GODS, THIS WAS A
PUNISHMENT NOT A RARE FIND?
FOR THE FLAME THAT BURNED NO LONGER
BURNED ELSEWHERE
I WAS OUT OF TIME, OUT OF HER MIND.
I WAS STUCK DOWN BY DIVINE PAIN.

SHE WAS, SO RARE LIKE THE DAWN OF EXISTENCE.
A TREASURE FEW COULD ADMIRE, UNABLE TO DIG
DEEP ENOUGH TO UNCOVER ANOTHER...
SHE WAS ONE IN A MILLION, AN IMPOSSIBILITY
YET A POSSIBILITY.
I RETURNED THE DIAMOND WITH GREAT GRIEF
REMORSE AND EXTERNAL PAIN,
KNOWING ANOTHER WOULD FIND MY GEM.

True Connection

Did she fall for me because she loved me,
or did she see and feel how I loved her,
Then she simply fell for me?

Our second chance almost didn't happen,
I told her how I felt it changed her
predestined decision.

I confessed, on the edge of fate.
I spoke from the depths of the heart,
Changing predetermined fate.
Eternity itself was shaken.
The gods turned; they paid attention.
As though my hearts truth, altered the
divines intent,
Altering a page in destiny's script.

A spark of existence fluttered,
Until it scattered reigniting what was
there,
The halls of the heart were lit once more,
Dark shadows were cast away.
We flew on the spiritual realm.
Transcending our former ties to the
earth
The gods gave us our time.

To bask in the stars.

Until we struck the earth again, craters
remain on a once blissful land.
Our stars crashed, burning bright to
their final decent-
Yet, time and need tore us apart,
Leaving remnants of eternal truth.

Perhaps our bond was unique.
Perhaps she feels and remembers as I do.
Perhaps, just because another likes her,
she wouldn't give them the time of day.
She feels it and sees it like I did-
A truth transcending mere presence.

Did she fall for me because she loved me,
Or did she simply feel and respond to how
I loved her?
If she falls for anyone who shows her
affection,
Does it cheapen the depth of what we
once shared?
Or does it reveal a truth that love can be
fleeting,
And true connection is rare and
profound?

DIFFERENCES

HAD I HAD MORE TIME, WOULD WE STILL BE
HERE?
HAD I BEEN FUN, WOULD WE STILL BE NEAR?
HAD SHE SEEN ME THRIVING, NOT MERELY
SURVIVING,
NOT JUST KEEPING MY HEAD ABOVE WATER, BUT
TRULY LIVING.
WITH POCKETS NOT INSIDE OUT, BUT FULL OF
LIFE.

HAD SHE SEEN ME OUT WITH FRIENDS,
EMBRACING LIFE
WOULD WE STILL BE?
HAD SHE MEET THEM, SHARED IN LIFE'S BRIGHT
MOMENTS RIFE,
HAD I BEEN ABLE TO LIVE, SHARING MY LIFE
WITH HER, WOULD WE STILL BE?
WOULD WE STILL BE, OR WOULD SHE HAVE
TAKEN FLIGHT?

I PROMISED MYSELF, WE WOULD NEVER CRASH
AND BURN,
YET OUR STAR HAS GONE DOWN, WE BOTH HAD
TO LEARN.
TO NOT LOOK FOR THE OTHER, ANYMORE,

We drifted apart, forevermore.
My compass no longer follows her star.
Lost in the distance, we've travelled too
far.
The northern lights, no longer shine
down on us.
Leaving our nights in a shadowed dark.
Travelling to worlds end, I remained in
the dark.
I travel unguided, lost in the fog.

In the distance over time, her star shone
again,
But why? It had been too long.
Was it a beacon, guiding me home?
Dare I chart my way back,
Or remain away, where memories lack?
She was my angel in the night,
Guiding me with her eternal light.
Now she's gone, I'm left to find
My way through the dark, cold, and
alone.
Dare I send a letter ahead,
Or stay in silence, where echoes fade,
Exploring the paths I've walked, delayed?
Her light is guiding me back, yet I can't
explain why; it wasn't her intent.

Different Paths

She loved horses- studied them, rode
them,
Their hooves thundering against the
earth with a blissful gallop.
Their grace and power, a strange embrace
It was her passion; it was her love.

I wanted to ride a bike,
Pedalling along winding roads,
Feeling the sun and wind on my face,
Chasing new horizons on two wheels.

She spoke of galloping through the
fields, under the sun.
The reins and saddle were a part of her.
I dreamed of long cycles and trails,
Riding side by side behind her,

We were united in our wants,
Intersections of mutual curiosity existed,
We would ride in country lanes,
Yet destiny pulled us in opposite
directions.
At dawn, our paths crossed.
I saw the, where we were,

I couldn't let this go on, no more.
I drew a line in the sand.
I had to be brave, and go our separate
ways.

I would compromise,
Ride a horse, though not feeling out of
place,
She tried riding a bike.
Both stepping out of our zones of
comfort.
In the end, we learned love doesn't ride
the same path.
Journeys can be different but still hold
meaning.
She rode away on her steed, out of my life,
while I pedalled through dawn chasing
my dreams, though they led back to her.

We travelled separate roads, our
memories I hold dear.
I needed no map to remember where we'd
been.
I loved and I lost,
If only I could give her the commitment,
we both wanted, perhaps we'd remain
together.

GUARDIAN

IF SHE WERE THREATENED, SHE NEEDN'T FEAR.
SOMETHING AWOKE WITHIN ME, GIVING AN
EDGE.
I WAS A SPARTAN, STRONGER, FASTER, SMARTER,
NOT A HUMAN BENIGN.
THE STRENGTH OF A THOUSAND MEN, SPEED OF
LIGHTING, SPARTANS ARE FORGED, NOT BORN.
I AM HER SHIELD, HER GUARDIAN ANGEL.
HER KNIGHT IN SHINING ARMOUR
IN HER DEFENCE I'D FEEL NO PAIN, HAVE NO
CONVICTION.
IN THAT MOMENT OF NEED, I AM A DEMI-GOD.
THE FORCE WAS STRONG WITH ME.
A POWER BORROWED, BY PRAYERS.
DRIVEN BY DELIRIUM ETERNAL, A DARK FATE
AWAITS THOSE WHO WOULD THREAT.
NATURES STORM SMITING THOSE WHO STAND
BEFORE US WITH THE CALM OF A STREAM.
THE DEMENTORS WRAITH WOULD COME FOR
THOSE WHO STOOD BEFORE US.
THE GODS WOULD STRIKE THOSE WHO OPPOSED
ME DOWN, WITH INEVITABLE INTENT.
THE MOMENT THEY THREATENED THEIR
PASSING WAS ASSURED.
FOR NO MAN, STANDS BEFORE THE GODS.

Should I fall, the force itself would sustain me, until she was away.
A mortal wound, yet I still stand and fight.
The gods give me their strength.
As though I'd drank from the grail itself.
Facing darkness, I walk towards my fate.
Time would cease to be, and mortal needs would be transcended.
I'd accept my fleeting fate.
Once she was carried away, safe I'd fall.
Power borrowed from the gods would be returned, the sands of time wouldn't change.
Queen Susan Pevensie's horn would be blown, I would be summoned away.
I'd answer the final call.
I had done my duty, beyond queen and country.
I'd enter the halls of Valhalla, to be carried there, burned on a bed.
Even in death, she'd not walk alone.
Like a phoenix rising from the ashes,
I was one with the force,
A guardian always present but never seen.
I will keep on fighting, till the end.
For, Spartans never die.

Questions Not Asked

A fateful day, steeped in infamy,
Long ago, still lives within me.
She asked, "what would you do if I were…"
I was taken by surprise, unsure how to
answer; it wasn't expected.
I was caught off guard, unprepared, the
question unanticipated.
She provided assurance she wasn't, but
why ask such a thing?
She assured me it was hypothetical, but
why ask such a thing?
I pondered her intent; I questioned the
reassurances.
The question lingers in my mind, to this
day.
Were it true, this day would profoundly
different.
I wasn't ready, but I would have been…

What I always wanted with her, would
have become true,
No longer a farfetched dream, a lived
reality.
It's something she longed for, when she
learned of something personal and deep.

SHE SHARED IT WITH ME; I WANTED THE SAME.
DID SHE ASK, BECAUSE IT WAS TRUE?
WOULD MY ANSWER HAVE CHANGED THINGS?
WAS SHE CONTEMPLATING KEEPING THINGS
GOING FOR BRIGHTER DAYS?
WHY DIDN'T SHE SIMPLY JUST SAY...

I'D HAVE RISEN TO THE CHALLENGE, AND DONE
MORE.
I'D HAVE SACRIFICED MY TIME FOR A FUTURE
WITH HER,
I'D LET GO OF ALL OTHER AMBITIONS.
FOR IT WAS NO LONGER ONLY US, IT IF WERE
TRUE.
I'D LOSE IT ALL FOR HER; SHE WAS THE ONLY
TREASURE IN LIFE, I TRIED TO MAINTAIN.
I HOPE I WAS WRONG THAT DAY, FOR I'VE TRULY
LOST.
WE BOTH DESIRED THE SAME,
WE WERE JUST NOT AT THE RIGHT PLACE IN
TIME.
IF IT WERE AS I FEAR, I'VE TRULY LOST.
NOT UNTIL THIS DAY, I PONDERED IT MORE
THINKING WHAT SHE HAS DONE.
COULD WE HAVE BEEN MORE,
IF QUESTIONS WERE TRULY ASKED?
I'D HAVE GIVEN IT ALL, FOR HER.

ENDS OF THE EARTH

IF I COULD TURN BACK TIME, USING THE SANDS
OF TIME.
I'D GO BACK TO CHANGE IT ALL,
ALTERING HISTORY AND TIME ITSELF.
I'D TRAVEL TO HELL AND BACK.
JUST TO SEE YOUR SMILE AGAIN.
FROM THE DEPTHS OF THE EARTH,
I'D CALL, CHANGING IT ALL.

THE HEARTS THAT SPLIT AWAY, I'D BRING
TOGETHER AGAIN.
WOUNDS OF TIME ALTERED AND HEALED.
WITH CUPID'S BOW, WE'D FALL AGAIN.
I'D UNDO THE PAIN, OF BEFORE.

WE'D CHART NEW PATHS, REWRITING PAGES IN A
PUBLISHED NOVEL.
OUR JOURNEY BRIGHT, GUIDED BY HOPE'S LIGHT,
WE'D REACH NEW HEIGHTS.

IF I COULD FIND THE SANDS OF TIME, I'D
CHANGE IT ALL,
I'D RISE FROM WHERE WE FELL,
ANSWERING THE CALL OF OUR HEARTS,
EMBRACING THE JOURNEY.

I'D MOVE MOUNTAINS, CLIMB IMPOSSIBLE
TERRAIN.
I'LL WALK THROUGH FIRE, I'D WALK ON WATER,
TO SIMPLY FIND YOU.
I'D BATTLE GOLIATH AND SUCCEED.
FOR THE GODS WOULD SEE MY STRUGGLE AND
AID MY PLIGHT.
DAY WOULD TURN TO NIGHT, AS THE CLOCK
TICKS BACK AGAIN.
GIVING AN OPPORTUNITY FOR US TO THRIVE
AGAIN...

YOU WERE ALL I EVER WANTED, NOW YOU'RE
GONE,
MY LOVE FOR YOU WAS STRONG, I'LL WAIT HERE
BY THE PHONE.
SINCE SEEING YOU AGAIN, I CAN'T BEAR TO
SLEEP ALONE,
EACH NIGHT'S PASSING, A REMINDER OF THE
LOVE WE'D KNOWN.
I'LL FOLLOW THE NORTHERN LIGHTS, TO FIND
THE SANDS OF TIME.
WITH A HEAVY HEART I'LL CROSS VAST
HORIZONS TO FIND A WAY TO END THIS PAIN.
IF IT SEEMS IMPOSSIBLE, ONLY ONE WHO TRULY
CARES WILL MAKE THE JOURNEY,
TO FIND THE SANDS OF TIME.

HOPEFUL WISH

YOU WERE ALL I EVER WANTED, NOW YOU'RE
GONE,
MY LOVE FOR YOU WAS STRONG, I'LL WAIT HERE
BY THE PHONE.
HOLDING OUT HOPE FOR ANOTHER
TOMORROW.
SINCE SEEING YOU AGAIN, I CAN'T BEAR TO
SLEEP ALONE,
EACH NIGHT GONE BY, A REMINDER THAT
YOU'RE GONE.
A REMINDER OF THE LOVE WE'D KNOWN.
I'LL FOLLOW THE NORTHERN LIGHTS, TO FIND
YOU AGAIN.
CROSSING NO MAN'S LAND, IN SEARCH OF A
LOVE WE KINDLED.
THROUGH WET AND COLD, HELL AND EARTH
I'LL ROAM, SEEKING A WAY TO BRING YOU BACK,
TO OUR ONCE-SHARED HOME.
I WILL DO WHAT I MUST, A MAN CAN DREAM.
SOMEWHERE OUT THERE, LIES A FUTURE WHERE
OUR HOPES AND DREAMS MEET.
I ONCE TOLD YOU I'D ALWAYS CARE, TODAY IT'S
A CURSE HAUNTING MY EVERY DAY.
EACH DAY AND NIGHT, A REMINDER OF YOUR
LOSS.

Waiting For You

You were all I ever wanted; now you're gone,
my love for you was strong, I'll keep
waiting here by the phone.
After seeing you again, I don't want to
sleep alone,
memories of you haunt my every night
alone.
Each passing day feels longer, nights
even colder,
your warm embrace is no longer,
your head on my shoulder, is what I miss
the most.
If I could I'd bring you to my side, so I
could always find you beside me.
Your absence, feels like a part of me has
gone.
You were my angel in the night; I
cherished our moments, more than you
could ever know.
Our memories cradled I shall never
forget.
I'll keep waiting by the phone,
for you are my heart, my love, my home,
you were it all, though you never felt it...

MEET AGAIN

If we were to meet, again where would it
be?
The pub, the green where it all ended,
In what sense?
Could we turn back time and start again,
Or would our time have been and gone.

I have changed, she will have changed.
For better or for worse, it's a day I dread,
For what if I wanted has already
happened?
Yet I invited her to reach back out, I must
answer the call.

How could I love her still when all I ever
wanted has already happened?
It would not be unique; it wouldn't be
our own.
You never forget your first, is what they
say.
How could I love her still when a
constant reminder exists of what I really
wanted can never be?
Could I cope, or would this be too much
to endure...

LIES

I HOPE SHE REALIZES THE CHOICE SHE HAS
MADE,
GUYS CAN BE CONVINCING, FOR FEW ARE
TRULY GENUINE.
MAY THE GODS BE THE DEATH OF ME; I HOPE
SHE HASN'T FALLEN INTO THAT TRAP.
SHOULD SHE REALIZE, IN SHOCK AND HORROR,
THAT TIMES WERE LIES,
ONCE IT'S TOO LITTLE, TOO LATE- TIMES GONE.
HER CHANCES OF FINDING ANOTHER, ARE
FOREVER DIMINISHED,
SHOULD SHE REACH OUT TO ME, STEPPING INTO
MY SHOES,
DARING TO REACH BACK OUT, WILL SHE SEE THE
TRUTH I HOLD?

SHE LOVED ME ONCE, LOVED ME TWICE, SHE
WAS BROKEN-HEARTED WHEN WE FINALLY
DEPARTED.
I WILL ALWAYS LOVE HER, BUT HOW WE
RECONNECT MATTERS.
I WON'T BE A SECOND CHOICE NOR A
PROFOUND CHANCE WHEN SHE REALIZES THE
ERROR OF HER JUDGEMENT.
I WILL NOT BE A MERE LAST RESORT.

FAMILY

A PAINFUL DAY STRUCK ME HARD, AS IF TIME
ITSELF HAD DEALT THE BLOW, DAZED BY ITS
FATAL IMPACT.
AN OUT OF BODY EXPERIENCE UNFOLDED, I
DRIFTED AWAY FROM MY DISTRESS.
WHAT DID MY EYES SEE THAT BURNED SO
FIERCELY? A RAGING WILDFIRE UNCHECKED.
IT WAS MY SISTER AND HER BOYFRIEND,
BOTH SO JOYFUL, CELEBRATING HER BIRTHDAY.
WHAT DID I FIND SO TROUBLING, NOTHING WAS
OUT OF PLACE.
UNTIL ONE DIGS DEEP INSIDE, WHAT IS
CONCEALED CAN BE REVEALED.
IT WAS THE MOMENTS THEY SHARED THAT SHE
LONGED FOR, MOMENTS LIKE THESE, YET I
COULDN'T THEN FOR LACK OF TIME—NOW I
FINALLY CAN.
I SEE HER HAPPY; ALL SHE NEEDED WAS
MOMENTS LIKE THESE.
SIMPLE BUT TRUE, OUR LOVE WOULD FLOURISH
AND PROSPER.
EXPLORING CELESTIAL PLANES OF
CONSCIOUSNESS, I PONDER HOW TO FIND MY
WAY BACK.
FOR I AM LOST.

She was a part of me, I was a part of her.
At one point in time, we were one.
We shared a profound bond, intertwining both physically and emotionally.
She was all I ever wanted, and I was hers.
I was all she ever wanted, and she belonged to me.
We belonged to each other, a bond unbreakable and true.
Forever linked, our hearts and mind intertwined.
Waiting for her to walk down the aisle It's what we wanted long ago,
I wanted even more; I sought something before that day.
We discussed it on the green, how important it was to both of us.
I never expressed that I wanted it from the very start.
At our first meeting, I felt a depth of understanding.
A feeling like no other was awakened.
That day, my feelings for her became profound.
I loved her deeply and imagined our life together; was it wrong to want this so much?

In My Shoes

If she were in my shoes, what would she do?
Could she endure the journey I've made?
Could she do the twelve-hour days?
Could she endure the journey I made.
She tried to juggle study and work but
surrendered; it was too much to bear.
She quit the job on campus, despite its
relevance to her studies.
She worked as I did but gave it up; she
couldn't cope. It was no way to live.
That was close to my own struggle, yet I
travelled great distances just be with her.
I don't think she realized the extent of
the effort I made-
I worked from dawn until dusk, then
journeyed just to see her face.
I think she appreciated the effort I made.
But did she truly feel its depth?
I did it all just to see her smile.
Because she was the one I was meant to be
with, I believe she felt it too.
Could it be that we were meant to be?
Perhaps the past was not the right
moment for us... just one more chance...

Hard Choices

One point, all I did was work and study.
I had no free time; money was tight.
I barely had time to see my friends.
I worked day and night, striving for a
better life.
I felt dull and old, as if life had passed me
by.
If I felt this way, what must she have
thought?
I think she understood it wasn't meant to
last forever.

The first time she accepted, the second
time I dreamed of better days.
Dark times fell, bringing a repeat of the
past.
A storm brewed, sweeping away all we had
built.
We found ourselves back at the start, a
place I dreaded.
Why must I endure this, god? What did I
do to merit such a torment, worse than
death?
Seeing her hurt brings me profound pain.
She didn't ask for much, yet I just
couldn't give, I truly loved and lost.

FALLING FROM GRACE

IF SHE WERE TAKEN, THOSE RESPONSIBLE
WOULDN'T FACE MERE HUMAN WRATH; THEY'D
FEEL THE FURY OF THE GODS.
EVEN DARKNESS CANNOT APPROACH ME; IN
THAT MOMENT, ALL LIGHT HAS ABANDONED ME.
FOR WHAT I SHALL DO, GOD WILL SURELY CAST
ME DOWN.
I SHALL TAKE MY PLACE AMONG DEMONS,
FORSAKING MY ANGELIC SELF.
YET IT MUST BE DONE; THE GODS TURN AWAY,
AWARE OF THE FATE THAT AWAITS MERE
MORTALS.
I WITNESS THEIR RUIN, DRIVEN BY THEIR
CHOICE TO FOLLOW HER.
I AM HER ANGEL, A GUARDIAN AND PROTECTOR.
I WOULD CROSS MOUNTAINS, TRAVERSE DESERTS
AND TUNDRA'S ALIKE, EVEN BREATHE
UNDERWATER; NO DOMAIN IS BEYOND MY
REACH.
THE MIGHTY KRAKEN DOES NOT STIR WHEN I
ENTER ITS SLUMBERING DOMAIN.
IT SENSES MY UNWAVERING RESOLVE AND
IMMENSE STRENGTH, AND THUS CHOOSES NOT
TO CHALLENGE ME.

EVEN DEMI-GODS MOVE ASIDE AT MY
APPROACH.
SENSING MY INTENT, THEY DARE NOT STOP ME.
EVEN THE GREAT TITAN'S YIELD BEFORE ME.
WHEN I CONFRONT THEM, SATINS DARKNESS
BEFALLS ME.
THEY ARE STRUCK DOWN WITH COLOSSAL
IMPACT, HIROSHIMA SHAKES ONCE MORE.
KAIJU'S SLUMBER IS STIRRED FROM ITS ANCIENT
REST.
THE GODS SEE THAT THE FINAL ACT IS
COMPLETE.
DIVINE POWER RELINQUISHED; I AM SENT BACK
TO A MORTAL PLANE.
ONCE DIVINE, NOW I TREAD AMONG MERE
MORTALS AGAIN.
I HAVE FALLEN FROM GRAVE, YET I ACCEPTED
MY FATE.
THOUGH I'VE DESCENDED FROM THE DIVINE, I
FACE MY FATE WITH ACCEPTANCE.
SHE IS SAFE, NOTHING ELSE HOLDS WEIGHT.
I AM HUMAN ONCE MORE, MY HEART BEATS
WITH LIFE AGAIN.
FROM AFAR I ONCE PROTECTED HER; NOW I
EMBRACE A LIFE TOGETHER.
FALLING FROM GRACE, WASN'T A FALL AFTER
ALL.

Now You're Gone

Now you're gone, I feel your all I ever wanted, more than you knew, you felt it too, you knew I loved you.

Our origins we must embrace, to continue our journey the way it was meant to be.

Without you, I feel cold and alone, surely you feel the same.

You were my northern light, guiding my destiny, forever me and you.

Our time I treasured, you felt it, but needed more, I understand we drifted apart.

Unending connection, yet we remain part, it doesn't have to be this way.

Remnants of you remain within me, never to depart, in time we reunite.

Eternity without you, is a torture I cannot bear.

Glimmers of hope, yet still remain, if you'd but answer our call.

Out of reach my love still burns strong, but for how long can this go on.

Needing your presence, despite the distance, we could be again.

Echoing forever, our love's enduring flame, you need only reach back out to me.

All I Ever Wanted

Always in my heart, even when we're apart,
Longing for your touch, though we're
apart, but not for long.
Lasting memories, keep our bond alive.
In my soul, I feel you there,
Every beat of my heart aches for your
return, don't you feel it too?
Voices of the past call out to me; I
cannot escape for it is me and you.
Emotions run deep in the void you left.
Remembering you is both comfort and
pain, I cannot let go, I'm not in control.
Wrapped in thoughts of what used to be,
dreams and future I've seen, for you and me.
All I ever wanted was to hold you close,
No words can capture how much I miss
you; you heard it and felt it yourself...
Through the pain, I hold onto our
cherished moments; I cannot let go.
Embracing memories keeps your spirit
near, now you're gone, you're all I ever
wanted, I am...drawing strength from the
love we once shared to continue on
alone.

Bittersweet Memories

I looked through the window of these
memories.
All the bitterness turned into the
sweetness.
Of knowing that I got to witness
What could've been and should've been us.

Now that you're gone,
I keep an eye on
Shattered glass on the pavement,
Like the Mirrorball hidden in a basement.
In the tiny house I built just for us in my
mind,
I go back down the stairs just to find.

This moment in time:
Timeless treasures,
Shiny feathers,
Of the endings, beginnings, and feelings
Brought by a bird in the middle of the
night.
It took away the darkness and turned it
into light.
Each day and night,
Every night and day, I long for you,
Now you're the loss of my life.

I still long for you.
That's how I knew it was true.
I sense the blues.
I follow the clues.
Back to the day
When I wished you could've stayed.

I trace our dances.
I lost all the chances.
I wander around the streets.
Just in case I can see your face.
But you're my beloved ghost.

Now that I've lost you again,
I'll preserve the memory with my pen.
To love is to leave.
To leave is to grieve.
I didn't want to deceive you.
Happiness is watching you fly free.
I couldn't give you the world.
I wish I would,
I wish I could.

Yet in my heart and mind, you'll always be.
An echo of yesterday.
Though we part, my love will never stray.

In my dreams, where shadows fall.
A hunting echo of our final call.
Your absence carves a cruel scar.
I cherish who you were, just as you are.
Through silence, I still hear your voice.
A bittersweet melody where we belong.

In the twilight of our distant past,
I find solace in our shadows we cast.
Through time moves on, we drift apart,
You remain a timeless piece of my heart.
You're in my heart, you're in my mind,
you're in my soul I feel you there.
You shouldn't wait for my sun to shine.
What was mine became a landmine.
I couldn't watch you die.
Now, this is a goodbye.
Now I'm at a cemetery of our memory.
We were legendary.

The greatest loss is that all I ever wanted.
Was what has haunted me for eternity.
Forgetting is like Armageddon,
But loving you was heaven.
I stayed true to what I told you from my
heart long ago, I kept my word...I would
always care...

Our First Time

On a soft moonlight night, we lay
together,
Entwined in a sacred space, just us two.
With movies on, their scenes a blur,
Beneath the screen's soft, flickering light,
Our attention was on the other.
I spooned you in my arms so tight,
Hearts syncing softly through the night.
I kissed your neck, then your lips;
You were safe with me, a gentle trust.
Before we kissed and snogged, our hearts.
A tender pause before we shared a kiss,
It made us both feel complete, at last.
You loved the way I drew you close, with
every touch, every kiss,
I felt your breasts, a fiery spark.
I sucked your breasts, drawing out your
moans,
Each sensation fuelling our deep, shared
desire.
Your breath faltered, a sigh of bliss.
We carried on; our spirits high.
I guided your hand down to me, where
you felt around with great care.
You later then,

Lowered yourself and took me in, with tender care, as time passed.
You explored me slowly, your lips and tongue,
You went deep; you did your best.
You made me wet, your passion expressed.
I pulled the leggings and then pants off, our desire clear.
I removed all your clothes, love's gentle call.
You lay back; I climbed on top slowly,
Stopping to admire you, staring into your dream filled eyes.
We both knew what was next,
Our breaths synced, anticipation and trust ever present.
I glided in gently, with no barriers between,
Every sensation heightened as we became one.
Intimacy passion and love had surrounded us swiftly.
I went fast then slow and then fast,
Our rhythm shifting with the beat of our hearts.
Your hands all over me, fully embracing,

Your touch conveyed the depth of our unspoken bond.
I went hard and fast, you lay there, gracing me.
Our passion igniting with each powerful thrust.
Your breath began to go, uneven and sharp,
Echoing the intensity of our moment together.
We reached a peak, I moaned your name,
I asked your permission; our moment drew near.
You gave me permission, and we surrendered together.
I filled you completely, our bodies entwined.
I filled you deeply, our bodies pressed tight.
Reaching the end, our breaths mingled, complete.
We cuddled and cradled each other for ages,
Holding the other close, as if to eternity.
Soon, we felt each other again,
I moved down lower, aiming at you with intent.

You watched as I played, captivated and still, enjoying the thrill.
I reached climax once more, over the entrance to you.
Our passion laid bare, every moment true,
Our connection intense, passion unrestrained.
We lay breathless for ages, loving each other,
In tranquil embrace, our love resonated deeply.
It was our first time, so pure and true,
Love was in the air, between me and you.
It was the best, for it wasn't just sex,
It was pure true love, the deepest reflex.
Shared between not one but two.
For true love and genuine real connection is rare.
Before long, we shared a shower together,
It was our first time sharing such a moment,
Romantic, true, and pure—my love for you shining through.
You felt it to, in the bliss we shared,
Our connection complete, in that perfect moment, so rare we were one.

Loss

My mind is lost, mourning your absence,
You were my life, our futures meant.
I was a part of you, you were a part of me,
we were one.
A future we both dreamed, but now echoes.
No echoes of laughter from children.
I never told you how much I wanted
children, to keep you happy.
The home we, imagined now a distant
dream.
Its warmth happiness, forever out of
reach.

Our dreams now shadows in the night,
Promise slipped from our grasp.
Friends and family, you never met,
My sisters you never came to know.

Our adventures charted, yet we never
took,
The maps we drew, lost and forgotten.
The family we imagined, a vision never to
be.
Ghosts of what could have been ruin the
night.

YOUR LOSS HOLDS ME DOWN.
EACH THOUGHT OF WHAT COULD HAVE BEEN
BREAKS MY HEART.
OUR FARMHOUSE BUT A DREAM,
OUR HORSES HAVE VANISHED,
ECHOES OF A LIFE WE DREAMED OF, NO MORE.
I WANTED THE SAME AS YOU- I WANTED
CHILDREN, BUT ONLY WITH YOU.
I NEVER SAID, FOR LIFE WERE HARD,
I DIDN'T SPEAK, I FOREVER HELD MY PEACE.
I DID IT NOT FOR ME, BUT FOR YOU.
I PUT YOUR NEEDS AND WANTS ABOVE MY OWN,
NOW I'M HERE IN PAIN, I LOST SO YOU MAY LIVE.
A SHARED LIFE – WITH ONLY ME AND YOU.
I'M OVERWHELMED BY GRIEF AND REMORSE.
MEMORIES OF A FUTURE NOW FOREVER LOST.
WHAT CAN A MERE MORTAL MAN DO?

WITH BUT HOPE AND TIME AS OUR GUIDE,
OUR HANDS MAY TOUCH ONCE MORE.
UNEXPECTED MOMENTS, A GRAND SURPRISE,
FORGIVENESS MAY FIND ITS WAY,
AS WE MAY LEARN AND GROW TOGETHER,
FREE FROM THE CHAINS OF YESTERDAY.
PERHAPS, ONCE MORE, WE'LL FIND OUR WAY.
AND IN THE END, LOVE'S PROMISE MAY RENEW.
AS THE PAST FADES, OUR FUTURE COMES INTO VIEW.

A Call Never Made

I could have stayed in touch, like you said,
But that would have meant, placing my needs before yours. That day a part of me shut down hiding you away.
I forgot because I had too, now I cannot forget.
My inner self buried you, in shadows of darkness.
I wasn't in control, I settled for less,
So that you could thrive, keeping my distance,
So, you could flourish, alone and unburdened.

I forgot because I had to, now I cannot forget.
For you are free, I can't understand why,
I am left with echoes of what was meant to be.
If I had stayed in touch, it would prolong your pain, for you loved me as I loved you.
If I made that call, you'd have answered my call today.

PERSPECTIVE

HAD I NOT ASKED FOR SPACE, WOULD STILL BE?
FROM MY EYES, I DIDN'T TREAT HER BADLY.
HER EYES TELL A DIFFERENT STORY.
THAT DAY, WHEN I SAID I NEEDED SPACE,
YOU ASKED IF IT WAS ABOUT US.
IT WASN'T. MY ASSURANCES FELL ON DEAF EARS.
YOU WERE WORRIED SICK, FEELING LOST,
KNOWING SOMETHING WASN'T RIGHT,
BUT BELIEVING IT WASN'T ABOUT US.

SHE WAS COMMITTED TO ME, AND I TO HER.
WE HELD A DEAR DEEP BOND,
EVEN IN DEEP FRUSTRATION, SHE REMAINED
COMMITTED TO ME.
I WAS HER FIRST BOYFRIEND, HER FIRST LOVER.
SHE WAS THE FIRST WOMAN I SAW A FUTURE
WITH.
I NEVER SAID FOR OUR PATHS WERE APART. I
WANTED WHAT SHE WANTED, YET I COULDN'T DO
IT-
NOT FOR LACK OF WANT, BUT SHACKLES OF LIFE.
I HAD TO SAY, YET I NEVER SAID IT ALL...
HAD I NOT SAID, WOULD WE STILL BE?
IF I HAD SAID IT ALL, WOULD WE STILL BE?
IN THE SILENCE OF WHAT-IFS, WE REMAIN UNSEEN.

WHY

WHY IS IT ANOTHER I DATED?
STILL REACHES OUT, DESPITE HAVING SOMEONE
NEW.
WE TALK ONLY AS FRIENDS; WHY COULDN'T WE
BE THE SAME?

MAYBE SHE BLOCKED ME BECAUSE IT HURTS TO
HEAR FROM ME,
BECAUSE SHE REMEMBERS AND FEELS WHAT WE
HAD, FOR ONE ANOTHER.
IT PAINS HER TO THINK BACK TO THAT TIME,
WHEN WE COULDN'T BE TOGETHER

I WASN'T CONTENT, NOT HOW THINGS WERE
BUT WITH WHAT WE COULD HAVE BEEN.
I HAD PLANS AND INTENT, YET BLOOD
DROWNED THOSE SWIFTLY.

I KNOW SHE LOVED ME, BELIEVING IN US.
WE HAD A FUTURE; HAD WE BEEN LEFT TO BE.
OR DID SHE MERELY PROJECT WHAT I
PROJECTED ?
SHE MIRRORED WHAT SHE SAW IN ME?
AND IN THE ECHOES OF OUR PAST, WE REMAIN
UNDEFINED.

STILL CONNECTED

DISTANT WE MAY BE, OUR HEARTS STILL BEAT AS
ONE,
FOR WE WERE FOREVER MEANT TO BE.
OUR BOND TRANSCENDS MORTAL EXISTENCE.
YOU AND I ARE FOREVER ONE.

WE MAY BE LOST, BUT WE CAN FIND OUR WAY
HOME,
TWO ONCE LOST, OUR DESTINY'S WILL BE
ALIGNED.
OUR LOVE HAS STOOD THE TESTS OF TIME.
OUR SOULS ARE ALIGNED, OUR MINDS REUNITE
IN TIME.

IN OUR DREAMS, WE SHALL FIND OUR WAY.
THROUGH SCORCHING TRIALS, GUIDED BACK.
THROUGH DARKNESS WE REMAIN INTACT.

WITH EVERY DAWN, COMES NEWFOUND HOPE.
OUR JOURNEY'S END IS WHERE WE SHALL MEET
AGAIN.
I LIVE EVERY DAY, KNOWING MY TRUE LOVE
WILL FIND ME.
FOR OUR LOVE SHALL NEVER FADE AWAY.
IN YOUR ARMS, MY HEART SHALL STAY.

My Love

Oh, my star light, you guide my soul,
Your eyes glimmer, guiding my way,
Your touch is soft and smooth,
In love's embrace, we shall stay.

Your smile, genuine and pure,
Melts my heart with every glance,
Your smile is so fair, a perfect cure,
Its pure art, I love in my heart's beat.

Your voice, every so kind,
Brightens up my day,
Your words melt me every time,
All shadows flee from your light.

In your presence, I am complete.
You make me whole, like no other.
Our union's tender, meant to be.
Our bond rare and unique,
Destiny itself bends to me and you.

We are bound by destiny and fate,
Our song was written long ago.
Our loves eternal, a flame that never
fades. Our bond will forever grow.

THE DAY WE PARTED

THE DAY WE PARTED; YOUR PUPPY DOG EYES
FILLED WITH TEARS,
IT TORE YOU APART, IT LEFT ME A BROKEN MAN,
BUT YOU DIDN'T WANT TO LOSE ME,
NEITHER DID I WISH TO LOSE YOU.
I HELD YOU CLOSE, CUDDLED AND CRADLED
YOU,
MY HAND CLASPED YOURS, HOLDING TIGHT
WITH GREAT MIGHT.
MY TEARS FLOWED LIKE RIVERS OF TEARS.
IT WAS THE FIRST TIME, YOU SEEN ME CRY.
I ASKED YOUR PERMISSION FOR A FINAL
PARTING KISS; YOU ALLOWED ME THIS FINAL
GIFT.
KISSING YOU ON YOUR CHEEK, KNOWING I
WOULDN'T EVER SEE YOU AGAIN.

YOU LOVED ME FOR YOU SEEN, HEARD AND FELT,
HOW I CARED FOR YOU.
I JUST DIDN'T HAVE THE TIME, TO COMMIT TO
YOU FULLY THE WAY I SHOULD.
DAYS NOW ARE TRULY GOOD; I WENT
SEARCHING FOR YOU AND FAILED TO FIND...
I HOPED OUR GOODBYE WASN'T THE FINAL
GOODBYE,

Mutual Intent

Sometimes one loves the other more,
Maybe that's me,
Not the mutual attraction of magnets,
Pulled together under natures will.

Once, our power was true.
Our flame burned intensely.
In time, it weakened but never went out—
That feeling isn't always constant for all,
Surely it fades,

Commitment follows,
A promise to one another,
Every day can't always be an elixir,
But a commitment is vow,
To cherish what remains,
Even as an initial spark evolves.

She committed to me, yet I faltered.
Now she's gone, I feel weight of solitude.
My soulmate has departed.
Leaving me adrift in this land.
Can't I commit to her, the way she did me?
I seek redemption, for times have changed.
I wish to rebuild the fragments of yesterday.

HIGH HORSE

TO THINK SHE SEEMED SO NICE- SO LOVELY, SO
KIND,
THE IMPRESSION SHE GAVE, PORTRAYED ONE OF
CARE.
YET SHE BLOCKED ME OUT, LEAVING ME IN PAIN,
SILENT AND DISTANT, SHE TREATED ME SO
POORLY.
I WOULD NEVER ACT IN THE SAME WAY,

TO THINK I HELD HER IN SUCH HIGH REGARD,
IMAGINING HER ALWAYS PERCHED ON A HIGH
HORSE,
HER STATURE CRUMBLES TO EARTH,
A FIGURE FALLEN, NO LONGER REVERED.
HER IMAGE NOW TURNS TO GREY.

YET NOW SHE'S LOWER THAN DUST,
A SHATTERED IMAGE OF WHAT I ONCE ADMIRED.
A REMINDER OF ILLUSIONS, I HELD DEAR.
IF SHE REACHED OUT, WHAT DO I DO?
DO I STAY NOBLE AND TRUE,
OR PROTECT MY HEART FROM FURTHER BETRAYALS?
DO I FORGIVE AND REBUILD WHAT WAS LOST,
I'LL WEIGH MY HEART AGAINST THE SCARS SHE
LEFT BEHIND...

Unending Love

Your simple smile separates insincerity
from sincerity,
Your eyes euphoric eclipse my gaze.
My heart humbles humbly before you,
In your voice, vivid verses of love are
voiced.
I validate and venerate myself to you.
My simple soul is yours.
I shall never waver nor walk away from
you.
I pledge myself to you,
Intertwined in intimate infinity.
Eternity as our witness. I am.
A loyal and loving protector.
A resolute and reliable protector.
My steadfast sword you swiftly
command.
You are my queen, my beloved and blessed.
My blood oath cannot be washed away,
A bond beyond the boundaries of time.
In your light, I find forever's flame,
A timeless testament to our eternal light.
As stars witness our steadfast stand,
All the realms bear witness to our bond.
For two lives have become one.

Pockets Inside Out

My pockets were turned inside out,
But no change fell out.
Just a wallet without weight,
With cards without value,
I was broke as a bloke could be,
Penniless, what am I to do?
I worked yet burned cash, you see,
And still had nothing left to spare.

I needed a break, my troubles prolonged.
For my family had betrayed me, it's wrong.
I was made low, like a beggar,
With no hope to beg or borrow.
I was owed but never given.
This debt ruined my relationship,
For it was never repaid in time nor kind.
For it was repaid, yet the hurt lingered
on.

I was taken for a fool, feeling blind,
The carpet ripped out from under me,
Deceptive deceit had burned me blind.
After all that was lost and undone
I face the future alone, overrun.
After her loss, I resigned...

In My Arms

On a quiet campus night, we lay together on her bed,
Watching the flicker of movies, with soft gentle light.
She set the mood, her lights turned a dim red.
Her head nestled close, asleep in my protecting arms.

We watched as "Free Guy" played its heartwarming tale,
And "Eternals" unfolded its epic tales of good and evil.
She drifted to dreams, with a smile on her face,
Trusting in the safety of our shared embracing moment.

The world outside oblivious, felt like a foreign land,
In that moment, our hearts synced as one.
In the glow of the screen, we felt the warmth of our bond,
A connection as enduring as the dawn.
It was a night I'll never forget...

History Defines The Future

If she knew me when I wasn't stressed nor
feeling down,
If she knew with time as an ally,
When days were long, and the world felt
prime.
Would she love me, and it never fade,
Has shadows of the past obscured our
shared vision,
Has the sins of our past,
Left a mark that cannot be erased,
Ruined and levelled the metropolis we
envisioned,
Destroyed as if by acts of sabotage,
The vision we created, shattered at the
seams,
The map we made, no longer guides us,
Our hummingbird flees us,
Is this how it's meant to be, just dreaming
of you missing me?

If I had the dial of destiny, time could be
erased-
Or would Vesuvius still erupt?
Will time mend what was lost, or leave us
in endless question?

Final Day

At a green by the river of a sea,
At the monuments peak,
We met once more.
Under the suns warm embrace
We prepared for a talk; we didn't want.
Our hearts burdened, answers to burning
questions were sought.
My eyes wandering, avoiding facing the
truth.
Words stumbled yet they found their way.
Through the haze of time, I found what
to say.
I spoke with truth and heart, without
fear of any remark.
In that moment, nothing remained in the
shadows being a mystery to you and me.
The air free and clear, as if set free.
I was broke, a part of me heart was ripped
away that very day.
Yet in pain, I found a way to cope.
Yet I never did let go, holding memories
close, come what may.
That day I lost you, I fell from grace,
I was in heaven no more, cast down to a
moral land with a heavy heart...

Chances Missed

I long for your embrace again,
For nights are spent alone without,
I long for your embrace again.

Like a great pain it doesn't fade,
Without your warmth I am cold,
Like a great pain it doesn't fade.

I isolated and cold,
This heartache, it has taken hold,
I long for your embrace again.

In dreams, your face I see again,
This longing, it has taken hold,
In dreams, your face I see again.

Each day without you brings only pain,
My heart in grief, my mind out of
control,
Each day without you brings only pain.

I long for your embrace again,
For nights are spent alone without,
As time goes by, I remain lost.
I long for your embrace again.

Natures Call

I was a wolf; she was a fox.
My instincts kicked in, yet I refrained.
For I saw something more than just a mere
fox.
Her eyes, glistening embers in the dark.
She drew my spirit in with ease.

I was noble proud big and strong,
She was virtuous, cute, and needing
protecting, preferring to be away from
her flock.

I travelled the lands, mingling with
many but never really staying, for I loved
my freedom.
Or rather I hadn't met one to cherish.
She was like me, curious and free,
Yet cherished her own time uniquely.

She was the one whom I'd start our own
pack with,
Having our own flock, in time, once she
knew me truly.
We were different yet wanting the same.
A flock and future to call our own.

I TRAVELLED ACROSS MANY PLANES TO FIND
HER,
MY PRIMAL INSTINCTS RETREATED TO SETTLE
WITH ONE.
WE MOVED TOGETHER, SEPARATE YET UNITED.
MOVING AS ONE WITH THE NIGHT,
NO LONGER PREDATOR AND PREY,
NATURE HAD BROUGHT US TOGETHER.

YET I RETREATED OFTEN BY NEED,
I HAD TO FREE MYSELF FROM CHAINS OF THE
PAST,
TO SEIZE THE DAY AT IT WAS TODAY,
TO EMBRACE THE PRESENT, BUILDING A FUTURE.

SHE WANTED NOW, YET I HAD YET TO BE SET
FREE.
I HAD AN URGE TO BE HERS, BUT YET I WAS HELD
BACK.
NEEDING FREEDOM TO BE WITH MY FOX,
THE GAP OF REALITY AND DESIRE HAD TO
CLOSE.
I FOUGHT TO BE FREE, BUT I WAS TOO LATE.

PERHAPS FATE AND DESTINY WILL BRING US
TOGETHER AGAIN IN TIME, ON A MOONLIT
NIGHT, AS NATURE INTENDED US TO BE...

FATE

Is it easier to love another?
Than reconnecting with a significant
other?
I reached out again, she said no,
But hearing my voice, her heart changed,
A new chapter full of promise enveloped
us.
Our history and hurt could mend.
If we but gave each other the time.

Is it easier to fall for a stranger,
Taken by thinking of a new thrill,
Or rebuild what was lost,
To heal yesterday's wounds, writing a
new chapter together?

Perhaps it's not a question of ease.
But one of courage and nobility to
embrace.
Accepting what was known then, and
what is known now.
Love is a journey in itself,
Yet our love was pure real and genuine.
We had something unique and profound- she
felt it too, if she was brave and embraced again...

FALL

SHOULD ONE HELP ONE WHO WRONGED THEM?
IS IT RIGHT OR IS IT WRONG?
WHY OWE A KINDNESS TO SOMEONE
WHO HAS SCARED YOUR VERY HEART?

DO I BE KIND AND RISE ABOVE IT,
OR DO I TREAT HER AS SHE TREATED ME?
SIMPLE WORDS MIGHT HEAL,
YET SHE LACKED THE GRACE TO BESTOW THEM.

DO I HARBOUR RESENT ME OR CAST A NEW SAIL,
LIVING ON WHILE FORGETTING THE PAST?
DO I LIBERATE, OR ANCHOR DOWN?
SHOULD I FOLLOW THE PATH SHE CHOSE,
OR DO I BREAK THE CHAINS OF RESENTMENT?
HER FALL FROM GRACE WAS SWIFT-
A LESSON THAT LEFT ITS MARK.
SHE WAS NO ANGELIC SELF, JUST A MERE HUMAN
PRETENDING BEHIND SHADOWS.
IN THE END, I SHALL RISE ABOVE,
I'LL ACCEPT FORGIVENESS MIGHT NOT MEND
THE PAST, BUT IT CLEARS A PATH FOR PEACE...
FORGIVENESS IS MY COMPASS, GUIDING ME TO A
HORIZON OF PEACE, THOUGH THE ONE I
TRUSTED AS MY COMPASS HAS LED ME ASTRAY...

ANGELS AND DARKNESS

ANGELIC YOU WERE YOUR LIGHT GRACED MY
NIGHTS. FOR YOU WERE TRULY UNIQUE, A LIGHT
SO BRIGHT, PURE, AND TRUE.
NORTHERN LIGHTS GUIDED ME TO YOU, AND
THEN WE EMBRACED, FOR WE WERE MEANT TO
BE.
GOD GRACED ME WITH AN ANGEL, A GUIDE TO
THE DIVINE.
EVERY NIGHT AND DAY YOU WERE IN MY MIND,
YOU MEANT THE WORLD TO ME.
I COULDN'T BEAR LOSING YOU, OUR LOVE WAS
PROFOUND, I SENSED IT, AND YOU DID TOO.
IN DESTINY'S NAME WE WERE MEANT TO BE,
PART OF A GRAND DESIGN, OF A FORCE BEYOND
OUR UNDERSTANDING.
NOW YOU'RE GONE, SHADOWS AND DARKNESS
ENVELOPE ME.
TEMPTATION OF DESIRES PURSUE, YET I STILL
REMEMBER.
HEAVEN WAS BEING WITH YOU, BUT NOW
YOU'RE GONE.
EVERY MORNING I WAKE UP BESIDE YOU IN
DREAMS, ALL I EVER WANTED...YET NOW YOU'RE
GONE. TIME ITSELF CEASED TO BE, YET IN
DREAMS YOU REMAIN.

One More Chance

Times have truly changed; I'd like one
more chance,
To know if we could forever be-
But not today,
But when you are free again and can
choose once more.
We'd have nothing to lose.
What could go wrong? I'll make promises,
I could learn about you all over again.
And you me,
We could start a fresh with positive aims.
What could go wrong?
Nothing to lose but we'd have everything
to gain,
I'd make commitments to you, if you'd do
the same for me...
I couldn't before, yet I can now.
It's harder to fall back in love,
When you've lost all love and hope,
With the right time and circumstance,
Our love could be rekindled,
Perception and reality could shift,
We could be again, if you believed in me
and you again...."if you believe, we could
rediscover a love that's meant to be...

The Day We Parted

Why was it the day we went to the park,
the day we were splitting apart.
Why was it the only day I wore jeans,
The day we parted ways,
By the Clyde at the green?
I spoke from the heart, I held nothing
back,
You cried because you cared.
About us, me and you.
You loved me as I loved you,
You didn't want things to be the way they
were,
You wanted more, yet time wasn't kind,
Time had torn us apart.
For dark days are truly behind,
Maybe we could be more once more,
And fly again, never seeking more,
Than simply you and me,
We cannot go on this way,
Me and you we're meant to be,
Your all I ever wanted, and now you're
gone.
Out of reach but never out of mind,
It seems a part of you remains,
Distant yet still holding true, I cannot let go...

How Did We Part

When it comes to you and I, the timing's
never right.
Now you're so far gone, it seems we'll
never reunite.
All I ever wanted was to see you smile.
All the feelings I have for you, I wish I
could share.
I'm sorry I couldn't be the man you
needed; so, I chose to let you go.
Maybe all we needed was some time apart
to grow.
I felt so lucky when you gave me another
chance.
Who knew it would fall apart in this way?

I feel so lost without you how did this
crash and burn.
Only for you does my heart continue to
ache.
For time will never tear us apart
I will keep on fighting for you and me,
For when we together we were all we
ever wanted
Our stars will never crash and burn...
We just one more chance...

Heart Ache

The day you left; a light went out in my world.
You were my guiding light without you my path has dimmed,
I did so much to better myself, striving to be the person you deserved.
I did all I could, not realizing that my efforts were slowly tearing us apart.

I couldn't halt it; the path was set, and I had no other option,
I gave everything I had, only to find myself still falling.
My path was set for me, my efforts, in vain,
Left with nothing but lingering pain.

My strength is fading, leaving me weary and worn.
How can I love again when my heart still aches for another.
I am stuck, unable to let go, though I can't fully understand why.
I need to move on, yet I'm trapped in a moment that won't let go,
Maybe time will heal, and I'll find my way...

Our Love

On a quiet night, our love shone bright,
A soft touch, spoke of what our souls
desired.
An endless desire, shared by mutual
passion,
Our hearts one, each desiring the others
heart.

In stillness of calm, our hearts love the
other,
We recall the love that once defined us.
Each touch stirs a memory of our souls
deep desire.

Time echoes our love, it pauses for us,
Her touch lingers in dreams, forever
present.
Our souls remember with unyielding
passion.

A soft touch from her ignites my heart,
A wishful soul reaching for what once
was our love.
Our desire echoes with a fiery passion.

In quiet, our souls call, for lost passion,
Rekindling our love, we cradled each
other close.
Every touch a rekindling of unfilled
desire.

The desires we kindled burn in the heart,
Yet our touch tempted and faded, leaving
just love.
My soul needs solace, memories of passion.

Our passion remains strong, though time
has passed by the heart,
A touch reveals remnants of our love.
The soul remembers the embers of desire.

Yet in the night of our shared dreams,
Our loves ember warms the cold nights.
Though time may break us apart, our
hearts align,
Forever bound by destiny's divine design.

Though our paths diverged, our souls
journey is forever entwined.
Every memory of the heart is affirmed.

You and I were always meant to be...

Never Fade

I can see you right there, staring back at me.
You're the one that I want, you're the one I need.
We were meant to be, can't you see?
There was only you and me.

You'll be here both day and night.
I made a promise to you, though I couldn't understand.
I wanted you more than I could bear.
I didn't understand I just wanted you and only ever you.
No matter where we go, our bond will always glow.

I know you wanted me to,
Maybe we'll have another tomorrow.
Just you and me
Where our love will never fade, for I'll honour the promise I made,

My promise held true, why can't it just me and you are again.
I told you I would always care...

Rekindled Emotions

Years have drifted by like the earth itself,
Quiet moments of the night,
My heart reaches out to you once again,
Reconnecting with what we held for
each other.

Our paths wandered, growing further
apart.
Our hearts beat in perfect harmony,
Time pulled us apart, like a flowing river.
Our shared dreams shattered, left behind.

I am here, yet years have passed.
Yet I still long for you, I don't know why,
Moments we shared, rare and pure,
I never forgot about you.

The love remains, never faded,
How can this be, time has passed,
Yet I still care for you both old and new?
Even years apart, my promise to you
remains the same.
You and I were meant to be.

To the past and the love, we still hold,
I promised myself I'd wait for you, I'm here now...

Bliss

One time, our bodies intertwined in bliss,
We paused, you knelt with a delicate grace.
Sinking low before me, you then moved with care,
Feeling your boobs in front of me,
Your hands gentle, your hands soft as the air.
You explored with a tender, rhythmic sway,
Guiding slowly watching how I looked at you,
Your lips, tender and soft with a whisper of heat,
You embraced me gently; it was so sweet a moment.
You caressed with gentle strokes, soft at the tip,
Sliding with grace, each motion delicate and graceful all the way down.
Your gaze met mine, a spark of deep affection and connection ensued.
Our connection, lost in the moment loving every moment.
Your hand moving rhythmically in a loving tender way,

I guided you softly, our touch merged
into one,
A unity of passion, soon the moment was
done.
You moved back, playfully teasing me,
Your hands caressed with a gentle ease.
Your big boobs in front of me
I drew eager, stepping closer.
You leaned back in, preparing for what
drew close to us both.
I moved with rhythm, intense and fast,
Before you, as your gaze held fast.
Breach quickening, you sensed the climax
nearing,
Your tongue out, a soft moan I heard.
I called your name as I reached the peak,
Guiding gently our connection unique,
Your mouth open, a moment profound,
I see the thrill in your eyes, where
passions found.
Our desires ignited,
I called out your name as I, in the heat of
the moment, your soft mouth received
the culmination of our desire, a moment
of shared surrender.
It was a singular moment, uniquely ours, where
true lovers embraced their shared passion.

SHE

IN QUIET MORNINGS, WAKING BESIDE YOU
BRIGHTENS MY DAY MORE THAN DAYLIGHT.
YOUR PRESENCE WARMS MY DAY,
IN YOUR EYES, I SEE KINDNESS AND CARE.
YOUR LAUGH AND POSITIVE ENERGY I LOVE.

YOU WALK WITH GRACE; IT AWAKENS MY SOUL.
EVERY STEEP A GREAT DELIGHT.
IN YOUR GAZE I SEE MY FUTURE WIFE,
I SEE THE KIDS WE ALWAYS WANTED,
A BIG FAMILY WITH JUST YOU AND ME,
A PLACE WHERE WE CAN BOTH UNITE AND BE.

YOUR SMILE MELTS MY HEART EVERY DAY,
YOUR RADIANCE BRINGS OUT THE BEST IN ME.
IN MY HEART, YOU'LL ALWAYS BE,
THEY'RE THERE IS AN ETERNAL FLAME, IT CAN
NEVER END.

OUR BOND WAS RARE AND PROFOUND.
YOU ARE MY WORLD, MY NIGHT AND DAY.
DESTINY AND FATE ARE ONE AND THE SAME.
WHEN YOU SPEAK, I LISTEN CAREFULLY.
IN YOUR PRESENCE, I FIND PURE PEACE.
YOU ARE MESMERISING AND PURE OF HEART.

Every moment with you, I feel like I am in a trance,
You are my angel in the night,
You are the light in my heart.
You are in my soul; I feel you there.
You are a treasure I cannot lose,

Time with you is unforgettable,
I shall never forget.
The times we shared, only you and me.
In your presence I embrace you,
For I truly love you.
In you I've found my forever after.

I wish to spend every day with you,
To share my life with you,
To grow old and happy as one,
For you are the only one I truly connected with and you me.
Destiny's divine is on our side,

As years unfold, our lives will continue to meld together,
I promise to cherish you, to honour this love,
To keep the promise, I made to you that day.

JUST A TALK

I'M WAITING HERE BY THE PHONE,
HOPING YOU'LL FEEL THE WAY I ONCE DID,
TO LOVE FOR ANOTHER, TO DESIRE
AS I DID YOU, WITHOUT REASON NOR WANT,
I HOPE YOU'LL FEEL THE SAME PAIN,
AND KNOW WHAT I WENT THROUGH,
I CAN NEVER LET GO.

I PROMISED MYSELF I WOULD ALWAYS BE THERE
FOR YOU,
MY LOVE FOR YOU REMAINS TRUE.
EVEN NOW, MY VOW STILL STANDS,
I'LL ALWAYS LOVE YOU, FORGETTING YOU IS NOT
IN MY PLANS.

MY DEVOTION AND INTENT ARE PURE,
I WILL LOVE YOU AND DO RIGHT BY YOU
ALWAYS,
OUR BOND SHALL NEVER BREAK,
THE ETERNAL FLAME OF OUR LOVE BURNS
BRIGHT AND TRUE.
WE HAVE A LOVE WHICH DEFIES EXISTENCE.
WITH DESTINY AS OUR ALLY, WE SHALL ENDURE.
THE PROMISE I MADE TO YOU, STILL HOLDS
TRUE...
I WILL ALWAYS LOVE AND CARE FOR YOU...

Always The Same

It's always the same,
Love's a never ending game.
Won't make it to the next level, is that a
shame?
The way I play, always the same.

It makes life better or worse,
You don't bleed, but it hurts.
When a wound becomes a scar,
Time doesn't take you that far.
That far away from someone like you,
You were the one and I had no clue.
If love didn't exist,
There'd be nothing to miss,
No one to kiss,
None of this shit.
Love, you piss me off, it was a strong bond
that I cut,
And I totally fucked up.

Yeah, it's always the same,
Love's a never ending game.
Won't make it to the next level, is that a
shame?
The way I play, always the same.

So, tell me, are you called a thief,
When you take her heart and leave?
She won't believe him anymore,
Even if he loves her to the core.
I gave her hurt instead of healing,
Never took care of what she was feeling.
She wanted all of me,
I wanted too many parts of me to be free.
It's like this same old song,
They're always getting it wrong.
What love has done with my life no song
could ever express,
I don't wanna be in love, I just want to
care less.
Care less about this thing everyone is
looking for,
If they could, they would buy it in a store.

Yeah, it's always the same,
Love's a never ending game.
Won't make it to the next level, is that a
shame?
The way I play, always the same.
The rules may never change, the heart
remains torn,
Caught in love's embrace, forever
confused.

Life can be so easy, but easiness is boring,
How much do you love this hard feeling
of longing?
This hard feeling of letting go?
Putting on a smile and putting on a show,
When he talked about her it made me
think of you.
Wherever you were, it felt like you knew.
Had your picture in my mind,
Suddenly sometimes I wished I could
rewind.
Love doesn't know this thing called time,
Hadn't seen each other in forever but it
still felt like you're mine.
I don't know why we lost us so many
times,
We were happy but never really fine,
Fine with staying together as long as we
live.
Was there someone else in your mind you
thought you should be with?

Yeah, it's always the same,
Love's a never ending game.
Won't make it to the next level, is that a
shame?
The way I play, always the same.

IT'S EVEN HARDER WHEN IT REPEATS ITSELF,
IT DOESN'T MAKE YOU NUMB; YOU STILL NEED
THAT BOTTLE FROM THE SHELF.
YOU CAN'T MAKE ANY SENSE OUT OF THIS,
IT'S AS BITTER AS SOMEONE'S LAST KISS.
THE KIND OF KISS YOU DON'T WANNA MISS,
WHEN THE LIGHTS GO DOWN, YOU'RE ALL
ALONE.
THE ECHOES OF LOVE'S LOSS, CHILL TO THE
BONE,
MEMORIES REWIND LIKE A BROKEN SONG,
A FINAL REMINDER, THAT LOVE, FOR ME, WENT
WRONG.

YEAH, IT'S ALWAYS THE SAME.
LOVE'S A NEVER ENDING GAME.
WON'T MAKE IT TO THE NEXT LEVEL, IS THAT A
SHAME?
THE WAY I FEEL, ALWAYS THE SAME.

EVEN AS I TRY BREAKING FREE THIS CHAIN,
THE REMNANTS OF LOVE LINGER, CAUSING
ENDLESS PAIN.
A NEVER-ENDING CYCLE, A RELENTLESS PLIGHT
I'M LOST IN LOVES CRUEL MAZE,
I WILL NEVER BE THE SAME AGAIN,
MARKED FOREVER BY LOVE'S PAIN...

Delay

Why did she wait, why did she delay,
Was she considering just one more
chance?
Did her hearts compass sweep, unsure of
fates next turn?
Memories good and not good,
The ship un-steady searching the soul,
In search of an answer,
Does she grasp the call or let it fade,
Time keeps ticking on, relentlessly.
Does she find a new hope?
Or does her heart still pain, and the mind
remembers,
Can she let go, or cling to yesterday's
memories?
The hesitation hurt the most...
Knowing she was thinking about what to
say or if to reply.
Yet a day later, I was blocked. The void
unbridged by words, the delay a wound,
unhealed,
Is it another chapter just turned,
In the pages of chances never fully explored.
In the pause where her reply was almost
born but then was lost...

Author's Note

Thank you so much for taking the time to read *Verses of Desire*. Your presence in these pages means the world to me. As you reflect on the emotions and stories captured within these poems, I hope you find a connection that resonates with your own experiences.

I invite you to continue this journey with my other works: *Now You're Gone*, which explores what I once believed I wanted from a woman and the adventures we dreamed of; *All I Ever Wanted*, a continuation that deepens the themes and emotions of my earlier collection; and *Crash and Burn*, a personal reflection on what I wished could have

HAPPENED WHEN GIVEN A SECOND CHANCE—
POEMS THAT CAPTURE MY OWN ADVENTURE
AND HEARTFELT WISHES ABOUT KIMBERLY, THE
SPECIAL GIRL WHO INSPIRED THIS JOURNEY.

THANK YOU ONCE AGAIN FOR YOUR SUPPORT
AND FOR ALLOWING THESE WORDS TO BE A PART
OF YOUR LIFE. I AM DEEPLY GRATEFUL FOR YOUR
READERSHIP AND HOPE THAT THESE POEMS
HAVE TOUCHED YOU IN MEANINGFUL WAYS.

WITH GRATITUDE,
MIKE REID

Milton Keynes UK
Ingram Content Group UK Ltd.
UKHW020853211124
451474UK00021B/1048

9 781445 215259